How to
Eat Better
and
Spend Less

How to Eat Better and Spend Less

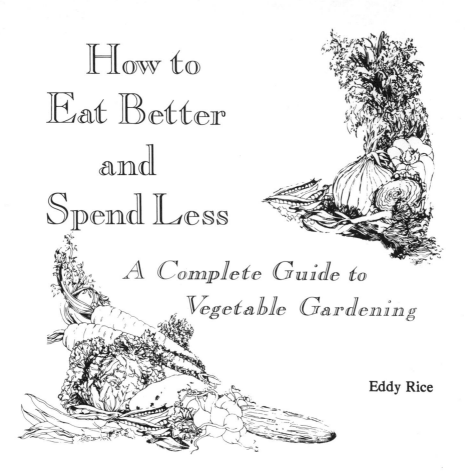

A Complete Guide to Vegetable Gardening

Eddy Rice

RESTON PUBLISHING COMPANY, INC.
Reston, Virginia 22090
A Prentice-Hall Company

Library of Congress Cataloging in Publication Data

Rice, Eddy, 1911-
  How to eat better and spend less.

  1. Vegetable gardening. I. Title.
SB321.R53   635   74-3110
ISBN 0-87909-346-3

© 1974 by
RESTON PUBLISHING COMPANY, INC.
Box 547
Reston, Virginia 22090
A Prentice-Hall Company

10 9 8 7 6 5 4 3 2 1

Printed in the United States of America

To my wife Dolores,
our son Jack and his wife Linda,
and our son Eddy Paul and his wife Ann,
whose enthusiastic reception
of the fruits of our garden spurred us on
to greater effort

Acknowledgments

The following companies graciously permitted reproduction of their material: W. Atlee Burpee Company, W.F. Allen Company, Gurney Seed and Nursery Company, and the Allcock Manufacturing Company. The United States Department of Agriculture provided the frost charts and much other specific information, including the various pictures of vegetables.

Contents

5   *Additional Vegetables for Your Garden*   97

Preface

There is a very old and popular myth that has to do with the idea of a "green thumb." Many people have grown up with the mistaken idea that one has to have special talent ... a green thumb, so to speak, in order to be a successful gardener. This is an absurd idea; nothing could be farther from the truth. Those people who supposedly have a green thumb are simply those with a bit of gardening experience or those who exercise sound judgment in following directions for soil preparation, fertilizing, seeding, and cultivation of plants. There certainly is no requirement for special talent nor prior experience.

Let us briefly explore some of the reasons for having a garden. A garden need not occupy a sizable plot of ground; an area ten by ten feet will yield a satisfying amount of fresh vegetables when utilized to the maximum extent.

Our first consideration is for the quality of fresh vegetables obtained directly from the garden. They are vastly superior to those sold on the general market, simply because you gather or harvest them from the vine or plant with no appreciable lapse of time before you enjoy them at the table. Naturally, they are in prime condition for best nutrition and flavor.

Now let us consider the sheer joy of producing our own fine food from a bit of effort coupled with an investment of a few dollars in seeds, plants, and fertilizer. Nothing, absolutely nothing, tops the feeling of accomplishment one gets from a well-tended and productive garden. This is true because it is an individual achievement; a personal experience; something done with your own ideas and your own hands. This type of satisfaction is hard to come by in most fields of endeavor encountered in our complicated and interdependent society.

Very few individual projects will give you the opportunity to exercise initiative, plan creatively, and reap such rich rewards as you will find in having your own garden. You will be very pleasantly surprised at the tangible and intangible results.

EDDY RICE

How to
Eat Better
and
Spend Less

1

Preliminary Planning

Economic Aspects

To put a dollar and cent value on vegetables produced on a small garden plot would be difficult indeed. However, one can readily see the savings to be enjoyed if one can harvest his own tomatoes, peppers, squash, cucumbers, and beans to mention but a few of the more common vegetables that are easily grown.

For those who do not have even one square foot available for a small vegetable garden, opportunities for gardening do exist. In the early days of our country a system known as "share-cropping" enabled the landless people to till the soil and share the rewards with the landowners. Today, many of our older people own good garden plots that they would gladly share with younger people who are looking for a place to grow some vegetables. One need not be a "special" friend of another person in order to seek a mutually satisfactory arrangement for gardening. In most cases, the only remuneration expected is an expression of appreciation, plus a few of the fresh vegetables when they are harvested. Naturally, these older people are proud and fiercely independent; so one must approach them on a sincere and equal basis. A sharing of the good earth and its abundant harvest can be a most rewarding experience for all concerned with the project.

The total cash outlay for a small garden plot can be kept under ten dollars for the necessary seeds, plants, and fertilizer—and this amount of money would not provide fresh store bought produce for a week for a family of four. So, if you are less than independently wealthy—or if you are an average wage earner with a family to feed—how can you afford not to have a garden?

Planning Your Garden

A garden plan will enable you to decide well in advance of planting time the varieties and amounts of vegetables to consider for the garden. Draw to scale the size of your plot and then accurately space the various rows of vegetables on it. Decide which vegetables your family really prefers and plant enough of each variety to make a worthwhile contribution to your table. It is far better to have four rows of green beans, two rows of staked tomato plants, two rows of onions, two hills of zucchini squash, and one row of pepper plants than to have fifteen varieties of vegetables and not have enough of any of them for a continuous supply during the growing season.

The garden plot should be in well-drained, deep soil that receives the direct rays of the sun all day long. While it is true that certain crops can tolerate some shade, no amount of water, fertilizer, or care can replace the sunshine that is needed. Even with a good share of sunshine, however, your garden stands little chance for success without adequate preparation of the seed bed. The soil should be spaded or dug up with a mattock to a depth of about eight inches. All clods should be reduced to fine soil and all stones, sticks, and other debris removed.

For a continuous supply of top quality vegetables from a small garden: work the ground early, fertilize properly, plant early, keep weeds down, thin for adequate plant spacing, harvest when vegetables are ready for table, canning, or freezer and then make successive plantings just as soon as the last vegetables in an early crop are harvested. It is not good gardening practice to hold out for the last two or three quarts of green beans if you need the space for a row of Chinese cabbage, kale, or turnips. This is but one of many such examples the experienced gardener can cite for you. To reap maximum yields from a plot of land, you must jealously guard use of both time and space.

Choosing Garden Tools

On small garden plots, one can easily work the soil into top condition for planting by using nothing more than a spade, a trowel, and bare hands. No mechanical equipment is ever needed on small plots of about 1,500 square feet. Nor does one need to invest in a whole array of garden or hand tools. A spade or mattock, a trowel, a garden hoe, and a garden rake are the only tools needed. For small garden plots of about 400 square feet or less, one can easily do without a rake and a hoe, since week pulling and cultivation can be accomplished with the trowel and bare hands.

Minigardens

One of the best ways to fight inflation and wage your own private war against rising food costs is to grow as much of your food as possible. If you are unable to have even a ten by ten foot plot of land, all is not lost. You can resort to a minigarden and grow a lot of vegetables in buckets, laundry baskets, cut-off garbage cans, window boxes, and wooden baskets; in fact, any kind of container that is large enough to hold enough soil to provide room for the root structure and nutrients for the plant. In these containers you can grow chives, radishes, lettuce, onions, tomatoes, peppers, and bush or snap beans. This by no means exhausts the list—almost anything can be grown in a suitable container. It is imperative that you provide small drainage holes in the sides of the container, about an inch from the bottom. Fill an inch or so of the bottom with coarse gravel or similar material. Planters for starting seeds may be improvised from egg cartons, produce trays, milk cartons, and other containers one receives from the supermarket. Fill them with top or potting soil and you are ready to start gardening.

You may obtain topsoil or humus for your minigarden from any woodland area or from almost any area that is being readied for construction. Most builders do not object to your helping yourself to a few bushels of topsoil, inasmuch as they are getting ready to bulldoze it away. Run your topsoil through a fine screen to eliminate small stones, gravel, and other foreign matter. Or, you can buy synthetic soil that is prepared from peat moss, vermiculite, and fertilizer. It can be obtained from garden supply centers and has several advantages: it is lightweight; it has the ability to hold moisture and fertilizer; and it is free from weed seeds and plant diseases.

The small holes in the sides of the containers, as well as the gravel or similar material in the bottom, are very important for good drainage. If the soil becomes waterlogged, your plants will die from lack of oxygen.

Watering and fertilizing plants and vegetables that are being grown in buckets, boxes, and similar containers must be done on a regular and continuing basis in order to have healthy, productive plants. When the surface of the soil becomes dry down to a depth of about one-fourth inch, it is time to water. The best way to water, of course, is to lightly sprinkle the entire plant, simulating a fine rain. During periods of dry, hot weather you may have to water your plants every other day. Let close observation be your guide. About a level teaspoon of 5-10-5 fertilizer to a square foot of soil is enough to keep your plants healthy. Mix the fertilizer into the top of the soil and then water thoroughly, after the plant is up and growing.

If your plants are in pots and boxes, they are readily trans- portable from porch to patio to windowsill. Remember that lettuce and leafy vegetables require less sun that root crops (radishes and beets), and that fruit plants (tomatoes and peppers) require full sun for best growth. Follow this general rule for all outdoor planting.

Soil

Soils are broadly classified as sandy, loamy, or clayey, with several types in each category, depending primarily on the amounts and types of sand and clay in the mixture. As a general rule, light soils are easily worked and retain enough moisture to grow vege- tables. In the event your soil is too heavy, it may be lightened with liberal applications of well-rotted cow manure or compost thorough- ly worked in. Soil too sandy to hold moisture and fertilizer may be helped by the same procedure used to lighten heavy soil. Small plots of undesirable soil may be excavated, carted away, and replaced with suitable surface or topsoil.

NORTH	Vegetable	Planting Dates
3 '	*Tomatoes, 5 Staked Plants	5-5
1½ '	Pepper, 6 Plants	5-15*
1½ '	Snap Beans	5-15
1½ '	Carrots	4-1
1½ '	Swiss Chard	4-1
1½ '	Beets	3-20
1½ '	Leaf Lettuce Head Lettuce	3-25*
1½ '	Dwarf Peas	3-15
1½ '	Dwarf Peas	3-15
1½ '	Cabbage, Early Plants	3-15*
1 '	Onion Sets	3-15
1 '	Radishes	3-15
SOUTH		

*Date to set out plants

Plan for a 10' x 20' mini-garden. Planting dates are approximate for the Northern Neck of Virginia. Refer to the tables on pages 34-43 for planting dates in your area.

2

Preparing the Garden Plot

Soil Testing

Much has been written about the acidity (sourness), and the alkalinity (sweetness), of soil. Fortunately, chemists have shown how to use the hydrogen ion concentration in soils to measure the relative degree of acidity or alkalinity. This measurement is based on the proportion of positive, hydrogen ions and negative, hydroxyl ions in the soil solution being tested. The positive ions indicate acidity whereas the negative ions indicate alkalinity. When the number of hydrogen and hydroxyl ions are in balance, the soil solution will be neither acid nor alkaline, but neutral—the same as distilled water. The amount of divergence from neutral is known as the hydrogen ion concentration, and the symbol in universal use is pH.

The pH scale for measuring the acidity or alkalinity of soil is numbered from 4 to 9 and includes the entire range of soil in which plants can grow. A soil with a pH above 7 is alkaline, or "sweet," whereas one with a pH below 7 is acid, or "sour." Chemical indicators are used to establish the known color reaction of certain pH values.

For practical purposes, 6 and 7 on the scale comprise most common garden soils. Most garden plants thrive in this pH range and are very tolerant of slight variations below 6 and above 7. The various intervals (measurements) on the pH scale are classified in this manner:

pH value	4.0 very acid (strong)	5.0 Acid
pH value	6.0 slightly acid	7.0 Neutral (not acid) (not alkaline)
pH value	8.0 alkaline	9.0 Strongly alkaline

There are several soil testing kits on the market that are easy to use and quite accurate. One of the better known is the Sudbury Soil Testing Outfit,® which comes in half a dozen different size kits and models.

State agricultural colleges provide soil testing service either free or for a small handling fee—they will test the soil and let you know the fertilizer and lime requirements for a group of plants or a particular crops. Your county agricultural agent has the necessary forms and pint cartons for taking the soil sample.

TO OBTAIN THE SAMPLE OF SOIL

In a garden plot, lightly scrape off the surface debris on the immediate site where a soil sample is to be taken. Then take a shovel and push it into the soil about 6 inches deep. Push the handle forward, with the shovel still in the soil, to expose a hole big enough to take a soil sample. With a tablespoon, scrape the side of the hole about 3 inches below the surface. Take 1 tablespoon of soil from this part of the hole and put it into the pint carton or whatever container you are using. Now withdraw the shovel and push the soil back in place with your foot. Take soil in this same manner from at least 15 random places all over the area, putting it all into the pint carton. This constitutes one soil sample.

Fill out the soil testing forms, being sure each area sampled is properly designated to avoid any confusion about area recommendations when more than one sample is submitted for testing.

When taking tablespoons of soil for sampling, avoid spots that are wet, areas where trash has been burned, manure has been piled, or excessive amounts of fertilizer have been used.Remember that your soil sample of a pint, taken from 1/20 of an acre—an area 33 by 66 feet—represents a tremendous amount of soil. The top 8 inches or so of this small section of land will weigh in the neighborhood of approximately 100,000 pounds. When you consider that your sample of a pint of soil weighs about one pound, you begin to appreciate the necessity for careful, precise, representative sampling of the exact garden area in which you are interested. However, if the garden area produces healthy plants with good yields when it is properly tilled, adequately fertilized, and generally well-tended, forget about soil testing—it is a superfluous luxury.

Fertilizers

MANURE

Manure is much more than a source of fertilization for plants inasmuch as it adds a large proportion of humus to the soil. This, of course, adds a lot to the moisture-holding capacity of the soil. However, unless manure is plowed into the ground in the fall, one should only use well-rotted manure in the spring.

CHEMICAL VS. ORGANIC

We need to "put down" a popular myth concerning vegetables and the food we eat. Some food faddists vigorously argue that chemicals are poisoning our foods and that chemical fertilizers produce vegetables that are decidedly inferior to those produced by organic gardening, that is, animal waste, manure, compost, and other soil conditioners. This idea has neither a practical nor a scientific foundation. Plants are not able to determine the source of the nitrogen, phosphoric acid, or potash they ingest and synthesize into nutrients. Consequently, organic and chemical fertilizers nourish plants in an identical manner and the resultant vegetables will be of comparable quality in both nutrition and flavor.

CHEMICAL

Basically, the complete balanced fertilizers are used to feed the soil so the soil can feed the plants. Cultivated soils are usually deficient in one of three primary elements: nitrogen, phosphoric acid, and potash.

NITROGEN

Nitrogen is responsible for producing vegetative growth—the development of stems and leaves. An oversupply of nitrogen will greatly increase the foliage at the expense of fruits and flowers. Nitrogen deficiency causes stunted growth, yellowing of leaves, and a decidedly lower yield of fruits and flowers.

A complete, balanced fertilizer with a high percentage of nitrogen (10-10-10) supplies the two other major elements as well as nitrogen.

One of the quickest available sources of nitrogen is found in 34.5-0-0. This fertilizer can be mixed with 5-10-5 in any desired ratio to increase the percentage of nitrogen. 34.5-0-0 is especially good around spinach and early season cabbage. However, one has to use this fertilizer very sparingly around most plants unless it is first mixed with a balanced fertilizer.

PHOSPHORIC ACID

Phosphoric acid is necessary for a strong root system, increases the vitamin content of plants, aids in early maturity, and increases the yield of flowers, seeds, and fruits.

The least expensive and most readily available source of phosphoric acid is in a balanced or complete fertilizer, such as 10-20-10, or 15-30-15.

If you are looking for phosphoric acid in a concentrated form, superphosphate is a common source. Superphosphate comes in various concentrations, ranging from 16 to 45 percent. When applied as a top dressing it should be thoroughly raked and cultivated into the soil.

POTASH

Potash is the third member of the big three and exerts a balancing influence on other plant nutrients. Potash promotes vigorous root systems and is essential for best yields and top quality root crops. Potash increases disease resistance and improves color and keeping qualities of fruits and vegetables.

A readily available, inexpensive, and highly concentrated source of potash is found in a complete fertilizer, 5-10-10 or 10-10-10, muriate of potash. Percentages range from 45 to 60. Rate of application is one pound per 100 square feet of soil.

IRON CHELATE

Iron is one of the elements necessary for the formation of chlorophyl. Most soils have enough iron in very minute quantities to provide for adequate plant growth. However, when these traces of iron are not available, leaves turn yellow and eventually go to a pale ivory hue. Of course, this same condition may be caused by other factors. But, unless the condition is corrected, the plant will eventually die.

Iron chelates (pronounced *key-late*) are used extensively by home gardeners for protection of valuable ornamental plants and shrubs that are suffering from iron starvation. The iron chelates may be applied to the soil in dry or liquid form and are available under several trade names. Directions for use should be carefully observed.

USAGE

You should shy away from all high-priced, small packaged brands of chemical fertilizers. The fertilizer one uses in a garden should come in a 50- to 80-pound bag and have a guaranteed analysis of nitrogen, phosphoric acid, and potash; 5-10-5, 5-10-10, and 10-10-10 are all good mixtures. The first figure is the percentage of nitrogen; the second figure, the percentage of phosphoric acid; and the third figure, the percentage of potash in the mixture.

Since most gardeners of small plots will be using chemical fertilizers, it is necessary to caution them with regard to the amounts to be used. A pound of fertilizer for every fifty square feet of soil is enough to provide nutrients for most vegetables; one pint of 5-10-5 is about a pound.

Fertilizer should be applied when the crop is planted or a few days before, taking care to mix it with the soil and to prevent direct contact with the seed. A bit of experimentation, coupled with close observation of your growing plants, will soon enable you to determine if you are using too much or too little fertilizer. Too little results in spindly plants and low production. Too much will cause the plants to shed their leaves and become barren. Placing the fertilizer so it will be two or three inches to one side of the seed and at about the same level of the seed will eliminate the danger of having seed damaged by direct contact.

Good yields of quality vegetables will not be obtained unless there is an abundance of available plant food in the soil. That is the primary reason for using fertilizer. However, you must be exceedingly careful in applying fertilizer around individual plants in order not to use too much and also not to get it too close to the roots—stay about eight inches away from stalk or stem and mix a small quantity with the soil in a small circle around the plant.

Mulches

Mulches are used to good advantage in conserving moisture, reducing the temperature of the soil, and controlling weeds in the vegetable garden. Anything that can be used to cover the soil without injuring plants or damaging the soil may be considered a mulch. Mulching materials should be inexpensive, readily available, and easy to use.

PLASTIC

Black polyethylene film is widely used in truck gardening and has most of the features that are desirable in a mulch. It is relatively inexpensive and will last for at least 5 years if properly handled. It is placed between rows or around stems of tomato, pepper, and eggplants, and is weighted down on the edges with soil, bricks, or rocks. The black color absorbs the rays of the sun and elevates the soil temperature—a highly desirable asset for heat-loving plants such as tomato, pepper, and eggplant. This feature also helps such plants to attain vigorous growth when they are first set out in the garden in the early spring. However, unless the film comes with perforations, it is necessary to slit many holes, evenly spaced, through it with a pen or paring knife so that even a light rainfall will drain through to the soil underneath.

This mulch is good in strawberry beds; it keeps the berries free of grit and assists them in reaching earlier maturity. Because of its

Black plastic film conserves moisture, controls weeds, warms the soil, and hastens maturity of vegetable crops.

heat-absorbing and retaining qualities, soil temperatures under this black film may be too high for some plants. Close observation of the plants, especially on days with high temperatures, will enable you to resolve this question.

HAY

Hay is a good mulch for the vegetable garden and may be used long or chopped for convenience. It breaks down into good humus, and if it is from a legume crop, it will supply additional nitrogen to the soil while decomposing. A layer of hay 3 to 4 inches thick is sufficient for a good mulch. This type of mulch frequently harbors mice. However, with or without hay for a mulch, mice are usually present in the garden. The mice can be eliminated by use of D-Con.®

LEAVES

Leaves are nature's natural mulch; these add humus to the soil, but they tend to blow away or drift with the wind into piles against the tallest plants. This difficulty is eliminated by lightly working them under the soil. Shredded leaves tend to stay put and the depth of the mulch can be made more uniform. In this way, they decompose and add humus to the soil much more quickly.

MULCHING PAPER

Black mulching paper is made in rolls of varius widths as well as squares for individual plants and is more weather-resistant than ordinary paper. It has many of the characteristics of black polyethylene film and is used in the same manner. Ordinary newspapers can be used to good advantage for conserving moisture and controlling weeds in small areas. Use five or six thicknesses and weight the edges down evenly and firmly in order to exclude all light. However, you must remove them to take full advantage of a rainfall.

PINE NEEDLES

Pine needles are plentiful in most area of the country and may be had for the gathering. They are weed-free and easily handled. They make an attractive mulch that may be removed at the end of gardening season and stored for use in following years.* Pine

*A layer of needles 2-3 inches deep is enough for a good mulch.

needles do not readily decompose and may be used for at least three years if properly handled and stored in a dry place. Although they are acid in reaction, they tend to shed water and resist decomposition. Since they are around your vegetables for only a short period of time, you will not notice any reaction in your soil or in your plants. However, hard and fast rules cannot be applied for all types of mulches and all kinds of soil in all localities. So one must experiment a bit, occasionally, and pay close attention to the results. If an acid condition of the soil should result from the use of pine needles over a period of years, it is easily corrected by the application of a small amount of lime.

GRASS CLIPPINGS

Grass clippings provide a good mulch if they are allowed to dry out for two or three days before use. When applied green, they tend to form a dense mat that air and water cannot penetrate. Apply the clippings loosely, after they are comparatively dry. A better mulch is composed of about a 50-50 mixture of shredded leaves and dry grass clippings.

OTHER MULCHES

There are many more organic mulches that are very effective, such as ground corncobs, sawdust, wood chips and wood shavings; straws, such as wheat, rye, oat, and barley; salt or marsh hay; sugar cane, and peat moss. However, all, except the last three named, extract nitrogen from the soil during the process of decomposition. This could deprive your plants of much-needed nitrogen, unless you increase the supply of nitrogen available in the soil at the time the mulches are applied. A pound of a complete fertilizer (10-10-10) per 100 square feet, or 1/2 pound of nitrate of soda, or a 1/3 pound of ammonium nitrate are the recommended applications to offset the nitrogen loss due to these mulches.

MANURE

Barnyard manures, when well-rotted, make excellent mulches for the vegetable garden and add both humus and plant food to the soil. Their nonavailability in most areas preclude their use by gardeners. They are invaluable for adding humus to the soil.

Top Dressing

Top dressing is the application of fertilizer, manure, or compost to crops without benefit of plowing. The beginner may get the idea that mulching and top dressing serve the same purpose; this is not so. Mulching, during the growing season, conserves moisture and keeps down the weeds. Top dressing is strictly used to feed the plant. The amount and type of top dressing used will depend on the crop. Top dressing is the most advantageous method to use on rich-feeding crops, on sandy soil, and where quick growth is desirable. When top dressing your vegetables, take care not to get fertilizer or manure on the plants. Scatter it lightly between the rows and in a wide circle around individual pepper, cabbage, and tomato plants.

Whatever material is used for top dressing should be lightly raked into the soil. Top dressing is the easiest and surest method to use for providing adequate nutrients for your plants. Heavy, continuous yields of top-quality vegetables cannot be attained without an adequate supply of plant nutrients in the soil.

Improving Soil With Leaves

Leaves are nature's tools for constantly putting back into the soil all the elements that plant life extracts. In addition to the big three—nitrogen, phosphorus, and potassium—leaves contain many of the essential "trace" elements such as magnesium, boron, and cobalt. These mineral elements are required for sturdy, vigorous plant growth—although in rather minute amounts when compared with the big three.*

Ever wonder why the topsoil in a deciduous forest is so rich in plant nutrients? This is due to the continuous and never-ending decomposition of leaves and other vegetable and animal matter. The top layer is known as *humus* and is the one ingredient most sought by knowledgeable gardeners. Humus acts as a storehouse for plant foods by slow release of nutrients and by prevention of leaching in extremely porous soils. Humus aids in soil aeration, in water absorption and retention, provides chemical plant foods while

---

*When one refers to "trace" elements it is with regard to the infinitesimal amounts needed by the plants, not to the amount of the element in the soil.

decomposing, and greatly improves the texture of the soil. Woodland topsoil with a large percentage of pure humus will absorb up to 500 percent of its dry weight in water.

Appreciation of the readily available minerals stored in leaves should cause us to stop and ponder the senselessness of burning or disposing of them as trash. Many people now use leaf-shredding machines to greatly reduce the volume and aid in leaf disposal. If you have access to the spoils from such an autumn leaf disposal operation, you are indeed fortunate. Turn the shredded leaves under the soil in the fall and they will be a part of it the following spring. Needless to say, leaves do not have to be shredded to be turned under the soil for decomposition. Shredding, however, eases the task for the small gardener without power tools and hastens decomposition and consequent soil improvement.

Leafmold added to ordinary garden soil—about 50 percent by volume—will add greatly to its enrichment and moisture retention. It provides an excellent mixture for potted plants without the expense of purchasing potting soil.*

Leaves are used in making compost, and as a winter mulch in strawberry beds and around shrubs. People in rural areas have always used leaves to line and cover the pits they use for winter storage of root crops, as well as cabbage and apples. The insulating properties of leaves have been used to good advantage down through the centuries.

Improving Soil with Grass

Grass clippings obtained from lawn mowing and turned under the soil will add humus and nitrogen to it. These clippings are of such small dimensions and are so succulent that they literally disappear into the soil in about two weeks. Given warm earth and adequate moisture, biochemical processes in the soil are accelerated, which further hastens decomposition of the grass.

Plan to work the green clippings into the soil as soon as they become available. They have their maximum nitrogen content when

---

*Flaky leafmold will provide the necessary organic matter for most potted plants. This consists of leaves that have decayed to the point where the integral parts crumble easily. This material is gathered from the forest floor and is readily recognized by its texture. Where there is a thick layer of leaves you may have to remove some of the top portion to reach those that are sufficiently decomposed.

first cut. Use plenty of clippings in a small area and systematically enrich the soil of the entire garden as more and more clippings become available for this purpose. It is well to bear in mind that most good garden soil is enriched and properly conditioned by man's efforts. The best garden soils are not often found in nature. Stop and consider: most natural plants bear only one crop per season. Nature provides for that one crop; and, where mankind has not upset her balance, she does a fine job. However, we must examine the other side of the coin. We expect our green beans, squash, tomatoes, eggplant, and cucumbers to continue pumping out their fruits over a two- or three-month season. In order for vegetable plants to give us continuing yields of top-quality produce, we must do our part in putting extra humus and nutrients into the soil. And we must go one step further to control the inevitable weeds, to keep them from stealing plant food needed by our crop of vegetables.

When grass clippings are being used for a mulch, let the clippings remain spread out to dry for a day or two so they will not mat or pack down. Then place the mulch around unstaked tomatoes, eggplants, and any or all of your vegetables to conserve moisture and keep down weeds. You will not usually have enough grass mulch for the entire garden, so mulch the earliest bearing vegetables first and the remainder as clippings become available. Put the mulch around plants and between rows to a depth of 3 to 5 inches. This mulch will stay where you put it and actually improves the appearance of your garden. It breaks down completely in one gardening season and should be incorporated into the soil for its humus content.

Green grass clippings are a decided bonus on the compost pile. A 3- to 6-inch layer under a similar layer of topsoil or barnyard manure will generate the heat so necessary for proper decomposition. Up to about two-thirds of the entire compost pile can be green clippings.

Green grass clippings constitute an excellent way to physically condition an unused plot of heavy clay for gardening. The green clippings are turned under the soil in large quantities; this is the process of green manuring—the plowing under of quick-growing succulent crops to add humus and fertility to the soil. When enough green clippings have been incorporated into the heavy clay, its physical texture will be much lighter, it will absorb and retain more moisture, and soil aeration will be greatly improved. When it has these qualities, you can grow vegetables very successfully on this piece of land.

Our vast and productive country has always been blessed with an abundance of good argicultural land. However, urban and suburban sprawl, coupled with our national obsession for more and still more highways, have gobbled up approximately one million acres of good farmland each year during the past two decades. This land is gone forever, with regard to food production. Looming big on the horizon is a constantly growing world shortage of food. Many complex factors will make this shortage much more critical as time goes on. I mention this here to stimulate your thinking about wastefulness and to encourage you to use grass clippings and leaves for soil improvement.

Nature, with her never-ending bounty for mankind, provides us with a seemingly inexhaustable supply of grass clippings and leaves. Their potential for physical conditioning and enrichment of the soil staggers the imagination because it is almost beyond belief. We have the organic materials at hand to build good soil from any plot of land we choose to work over. The question is, will we, as responsible individuals, make the necessary effort?

Compost

Compost is the man-made substitute for manure. It consists of fermented and decomposed organic matter, such as leaves, grass clippings, straws, vegetable refuse, weeds (either green or dry), peat moss, all types of animal manures, muck, and sand. Chemicals are added to aid in the decomposition and to add fertility to the compost. Composting is the easiest way to dispose of garden trash, lawn clippings, and leaves. It is also the simplest and least expensive way to add humus to the garden soil and improve its texture and fertility. Properly composted fresh organic matter yields a decidedly superior soil that is rich in plant nutrients and very high in humus content.

MAKING A COMPOST PILE

The decomposition of organic matter is due to the activity of microorganisms that are present in all healthy soils. So, to ensure bacterial action and a rapid rate of decomposition, alternate thin layers of topsoil with the organic matter.

Building a compost pile is a simple matter and its location will be

Making a new compost pile.

largely dictated by one's surroundings. However, a partially shaded area is preferable to one in the full sun simply because a more even moisture content is easier to maintain. As you build the compost pile, keep it from 4 to 6 feet in width so that you can occasionally rebuild the pile by forking or turning the outer portion of the old pile into the center of the new pile. On the bottom of the pile place a 6- to 12-inch layer of leaves, grass clippings, weeds, or garden trash. Tramp this layer down well to compress it and then sprinkle either ammonium sulfate or ammonium nitrate on top of it. Use about 1/2 cup of either of these activators to a square yard of area, and water it well. Then add a 6-inch layer of manure and a 2-inch layer of topsoil. Water these first three layers until the growing pile is thoroughly moistened. This process of alternate layering of organic matter, manure, and topsoil is repeated until the pile is about 4 feet high—with a covering of topsoil. Be sure to add the chemical activator to each layer of organic material.*

   If manure cannot be obtained, construct your compost pile with alternate layers of fresh organic matter and topsoil. The yield from

*The compost pile should be shaped like a pyramid so that it will shed rain.

such a pile will be just as good an additive as barnyard manure to your garden soil.

A mixed fertilizer (5-10-10, or similar) applied at a rate of 3 cups per square yard is an excellent activator for the organic matter.

Do not put twigs or woody materials into the compost pile. Keep the pile moist at all times. Decomposition is accelerated by heat and moisture. The chemical activators hasten bacterial action and greatly assist in fermentation and decomposition of organic matter. The time from the start of the pile until everything is decomposed and ready to use will vary from three to six months. This variance in time is due to materials used, temperature, moisture, and turning the pile over at 4- to 6-week intervals.

Alternate, thin layers of shredded leaves, grass clippings, and topsoil, plus a suitable chemical activator, kept properly moistened and turned two or three times, will yield excellent humus in three or four months.

The compost pile may be enclosed for aesthetic reasons. It also may be covered (to advantage) with black plastic to increase the temperature inside the pile. You do not have to build a compost pile 6 feet wide and 4 feet high in a single day—or ever, for that matter. Start with whatever is available and use the proper procedure for layering, chemical activator, moisture, and top layer of soil. Then continue to build the pile as additional materials become available.

The addition of barnyard manure to garden soils tends to lighten heavy, clayey soils and vastly improve the texture and moisture retention qualities of light, sandy soils; it also improves soil aeration and assists bacterial activity. Controlled experiments by several state agricultural extensions have proved that mineral fertilizers are much more effective when applied after an application of humus or well-rotted manure. Yields have been increased by as much as 30 percent when humus (or manure) and mineral fertilizers were both used. Used alone, doubling the amount of either one does not have the same effect on crop yields.

EARTHWORMS FOR COMPOST

The small gardener can enjoy the benefits of a superior compost by profiting from the activities of earthworms confined to boxes. Earthworm manure is known as *castings*. Earthworm castings are finely granulated and are far superior to other manures.

Either construct or obtain wooden boxes that are 2- to 3-feet square and 2-1/2 feet deep. Fill the boxes to a depth of 2 feet with a mixture of about 75 percent of shredded leaves and grass clippings. Add about 15 percent of barnyard or chicken manure. Then add about 10 percent of good topsoil. If you cannot obtain manure, substitute table garbage. Mix the materials thoroughly and moisten until the mixture is damp.

Purchase breeding worms or go out and dig your own. You must feed the worms. Dry cornmeal mixed with coffee grounds in a 1-to-3 ratio makes good food for earthworms. Dry oatmeal mixed with coffee grounds and any grain can also be ground and used.

The castings in the bottom of the box will get blacker and blacker. This material is finely granulated and bears no resemblance to the mixture you put into the box. About every two months you can remove these castings and replace their volume with your favorite earthworm box filling mixture.

Earthworms thrive under many different types and combinations of soils and moisture. The combinations of materials and foods for successful earthworm composting are seemingly endless. Experiment and closely observe your results. The main points to bear in mind are food and moisture. (Do not keep them wet, just a little damp.)

Lime

The many types of lime on the market tend to confuse the gardener. Horticultural hydrated lime, ground limestone, or ground dolomitic limestone are best for the garden.

Lime is used primarily by the gardener to sweeten the soil by lowering the acidity. But lime has several beneficial side effects, such as loosening the granular structure of clay soils, accelerating bacterial action, aiding in decomposition of organic matter, and supplying some calcium.

Indiscriminate use of lime is to be avoided. It is not required as an additive to all soils. It is not a fertilizer even though it does add calcium as a nutrient. The intended use is to correct soil acidity, and for this purpose it is superbly effective. Lime tends to release some of the phosphorus and potash from their insoluble compounds, making them available for plant food. Thus, in fact, it does enhance the fertility of the soil.

The usual prescription for general liming of cropland that has become too acid is a ton of lime per acre. Some authorities maintain that this ton-per-acre formula applies only to ground limestone and dolomitic limestone and that when hydrated lime is used, 80 percent of a ton per acre is enough.

The ton-per-acre formula, translated for the gardener, means applying about a half-pound per square yard of soil. Measuring is not necessary if you use care in spreading the lime thinly and evenly, applying just enough to completely whiten the ground.

Either fall or early spring applications of lime are satisfactory. Spread it thinly and evenly on a windless day, preferably on freshly cultivated soil. If not on freshly cultivated soil, either rake, harrow, or disk it into the soil. Spread it evenly and thoroughly because there is no noticeable lateral action. The effects will last for about five years.

Green Manuring

Green manuring is the term used to describe the turning under of quick-growing succulent crops. The green plants decay quite rapidly, thereby incorporating humus and plant nutrients into the soil. Green manuring is preferable and more effective than composting because the green crops are turned under when they are at their peak of plant nutrient content. Green manure crops should be turned under the soil when they are two-thirds to three-quarters grown and still succulent. Young, tender plants will decompose much quicker than full-grown, tougher plants. When the weather is warm and the soil has an adequate supply of moisture, almost complete decomposition occurs within 6 to 8 weeks.

Nothing is superior to green manure crops for conditioning soil, adding humus, and maintaining fertility. It is also the quickest, easiest, and least expensive way to accomplish these objectives.

It is an almost impossible task to compost enough materials to provide for the requirements of a large garden. The answer here is to use part of the garden area to grow a green manure crop and to rotate this green manuring each year so that it eventually covers the entire garden plot.

Some of the best green manure crops are the nitrogen gatherers, such as the legumes, which absorb nitrogen from the air and then add it to the soil. These legumes include alfalfa, clover, cowpeas, field peas, soybeans, and the different varieties of vetch.

Green manuring does things for the soil that are impossible to accomplish by composting, fertilizing, or plowing under barnyard manure. The roots of green manure plants penetrate the soil quite deeply and provide a good source of organic matter. The cowpea has a root system powerful enough to crack hardpans. (Hardpans are hard layers of earth beneath the soil composed mainly of clay and impervious to water.) Alfalfa regularly sends roots down to a depth of three feet in two years time. As the roots decay, they add humus and provide channels for aeration of the soil. This minute channeling of the subsoil also increases the amount of water it receives and retains. The action of bacteria and fungi, the microorganisms that make fertile soil a living, breathing medium for earthworms and other soil-building entities, is greatly increased or even initiated by the green manurng.

Long before the relationship between leguminous cover crops and their ability to add nitrogen to the soil was understood, the plowing under of these crops was known to have a tremendous impact on the fertility of the soil. It is now known that such a crop—plowed under while still succulent and before it reaches maturity—can add as much nitrogen to an acre as would the application of 12 to 15 tons of barnyard manure.

Cover Crop

A *cover crop,* as the name implies, is planted primarily to cover the ground and to prevent erosion by holding the soil in place. The subsequent addition of humus to the soil is also a matter for prime consideration.

Good winter cover crops are wheat, rye, the various vetches, and rye grass. These cover crops have large fibrous root systems that also add humus to the soil when they are plowed or tilled under. Good summer cover crops are buckwheat, soybeans, millet, and sudan grass.

Cover crops are used both winter and summer to prevent soil erosion, to maintain soil fertility by encouraging constant bacterial and fungial action, which is concomitant with all plant growth, and finally, to incorporate humus and plant nutrients into the soil, when turned under.

As with green manuring, you have a choice of nonleguminous or leguminous cover crops. The choice should depend on whether you want to add extra nitrogen to the soil along with the organic matter. And, for both winter and summer cover crops, one has to choose a variety adapted to the temperature range of these seasons.

There is one cover crop that can be grown successfully on poor subsoil or even on landfill, although several crops will add enough humus to the soil to make it fertile enough to support a vegetable garden. This crop is ordinary buckwheat. Successive crops of buckwheat turned under will incorporate humus into the soil and greatly increase its water retention. Sandy and light soils deficient in humus will not hold much moisture. Heavy, clayey soils devoid of humus will not support vegetable plants.

The procedure for building poor or acid soil into a suitable garden plot is quite simple. First plow the weed crop under and let the furrows stand as they are for two weeks. Then disk or rake the area smooth and sow a very thick crop of buckwheat. When the buckwheat is about 8-10 inches high, turn it under. Wait 10-14 days and sow another crop of buckwheat. Plow this second crop under when it is 8-10 inches high. In 10-14 days sow another crop of buckwheat. Keep this rotation of buckwheat going until enough humus has been added to the soil or until you want to increase the fertility with one of the leguminous green manure crops. You will be pleasantly surprised to note that each succeeding crop of buckwheat grows much better than the last. This increase in rate of growth is due to the humus you have been adding to the soil with each crop turned under.

Organic Gardening

Organic gardening is a system of maintaining soil fertility by the constant addition of humus. Organic materials are used for composting and mulching in an effort to duplicate nature's own way of maintaining and increasing the texture and the fertility of the soil.

Various compositions of rocks are sources of fertilizer for the organic gardener. The rocks must be finely ground or pulverized in order to become soluble and release their plant nutrients. Raw ground phosphate rock, pulverized limestone, and granite dust are all sources of plant food.

The proponents of organically grown foods are merely expressing a desire for garden produce that is free of chemicals. They do not approve of the use of chemical fertilizers and poisonous insecticides on garden crops. Furthermore, these same people do not think much of the food processing chemicals that are used for coloring and preservation in so much of our canned and dry foods.

There can be no quarrel with their tenets of what is good for the maintenance of soil texture and fertility. Humus is nature's own method of building topsoil. Nor can we question the quality of organically grown produce. The real problem occurs when one tries to envision enough compost and barnyard manure to fertilize the entire agricultural production of the United States.

Knowledgeable people in the Department of Agriculture have recently estimated that we could not feed more than three-quarters of our population if the use of chemical fertilizers and insecticides were suddenly banned from further use—a sobering thought.

Unless one has access to an almost unlimited source of organic materials or maintains an exceptionally large compost pile, the cost of organic material can be prohibitive. For example, 50 lb. bags of composted sheep and cow manure cost $2.50 apiece. The guaranteed analysis of available nitrogen, phosphoric acid, and potash is 1 percent each. By way of comparison, an 80 lb. bag of 10-10-10, a balanced chemical fertilizer, sells for $3.60 and has a guaranteed analysis of 10 percent each of available nitrogen, phosphoric acid, and potash.

It is my understanding that the Department of Agriculture is doing extensive experimental work in trying to develop plants that will act as "attractors" for insects that damage vegetable plants. The idea is to develop a plant that provides better food and protection for the insect than it is accustomed to having on its favorite vegetable plant. When this occurs, it is expected that the insect will abandon its favorite vegetable plant and take up residence on the new plant. These "host" plants would be grown alongside the vegetable plants they are protecting.

Protecting the Garden Plot

A fence sufficiently high and close-woven to keep out rabbits, chickens, dogs, and other animals is necessary to protect one's vegetables. The sides may be used as trellis (support) for peas, pole beans, and cucumbers. However, although this is a good preventative device, you must know what to do when animals manage to get into your garden.

MOLE DAMAGE

Many people contend that moles are harmless, even beneficial to the gardener, because they help aerate the soil in their ceaseless quest for insects and worms. Perhaps it is true that moles do not eat the roots and bulbs of your plants, but in their frenzied tunneling for food just beneath the surface, they do a lot of damage to plants by burrowing under and around the plants and causing the soil to dry out around the roots. The primary damage is caused by plant roots being dislodged and exposed to air, causing loss of moisture. Furthermore, it is a well-known fact that field and pine mice use the mole runs to sally forth and do their bit of damage by destroying newly planted seeds and young plants. In order to get rid of the moles, it becomes necessary to either eliminate or drastically reduce their supply of food. In other words, you must treat the soil with a pesticide that will kill the insects and worms on which the moles depend for their supply of fresh food. As soon as their supply of insects and worms is drastically reduced, the moles will abandon the area and seek out better living quarters in which to satisfy their voracious appetites.

Chlordane 10-G is a pesticide that is used to control Japanese beetle grubs, wireworms, white fringe beetles, chinch bugs, chiggers, ticks, ants, sowbugs, millipedes, sod webworm, armyworm, boxelder bugs, cutworms, white grubs, mole crickets, and earwigs. Some of these soil pests may be controlled for as long as four to five years by a single application of Chlordane 10-G. However, you must follow the directions on the label exactly because this product is toxic to fish and wildlife.

Small areas that have recently become infested with moles can usually be effectively cleared out by the liberal use of Mole-Nots. Mole-Nots are acorn-sized packages of tiny pellets that contain an active ingredient of 1 percent of Thallium Sulphate. They are effective when used according to the directions on the package.

If you have a very small garden area or seedbed in an area adjacent to mole territory over which you have no control, it may become necessary for you to physically block the moles from entering your domain. Simply enclose your garden area with hardware cloth, sheet metal, or discarded plywood. This barrier should extend downward from the surface for at least twelve inches and then extend outward at an angle of ninety degrees for another twelve inches. For the barrier to be effective, all connections must be secure and present no holes for entry.

CONTROL OF MICE

Areas of the garden or lawn that are interlaced with mole runs and frequented by field or pine mice will need to be treated for control of the mice as well as the moles. Fortunately, this can be accomplished quite easily by waging war on the mice with D-con®

The manufacturers of D-con® provide explicit directions for your successful campaign against the mice.

RODENT DAMAGE

Various kinds of rodents damage garden crops throughout the country. The extent of damage depends on the size of the garden, the type of control being used, and the numbers and kinds of rodents in the immediate vicinity. If you find yourself faced with a seemingly insurmountable rodent or mole infestation, your best bet is to immediately contact the county extension agent for assistance. These people are experts on local rodent control problems.

HOW TO DENY ANIMALS THE PROTECTION OF THEIR BURROWS

Here is a sure method of forcing any small animal out of its burrow or hole in the ground. You will need a 15-foot piece of garden hose, a small funnel, and about a pint of gasoline. Insert the hose into the hole by twisting and pushing to get it around the various turns and bends in the burrow. Now, hold the end of the hose about 3 feet above the ground, and, using the funnel, pour about a cup of gasoline down inside the hose. Remove the funnel quickly and press your lips tightly to the end of the hose; blow into the hose as strongly as possible. Repeat this hard blowing into the hose at least two more times during the next 15 seconds. Then drop the hose and hold a gunny sack over the entrance to catch the animal as it comes running out. Or you may want to dispatch it with a shotgun.

Once you start pouring gasoline down the hose, you must work fast because some animals will emerge within 30 seconds. The speed will depend primarily on the size of the burrow, the amount of gasoline vapor readily generated, and the disposition of the animal.

You can make an excellent bag for catching animals at the burrow entrance by cutting the bottom out of a burlap sack and attaching it to the top of a similar sack. Fasten a hoop of stiff wire to the mouth of the bag to hold it open over the entrance.

If you merely want the animal to abandon a particular burrow, force it out with gasoline fumes and then plug the entrance with anything at hand. Pour a little kerosene around the entrance. In most instances, these measures discourage the animal to the point where it will leave the immediate vicinity.

It is not essential that the hose reach the end of the burrow. However, the closer it is to the end, the quicker you can deliver an intolerable concentration of gasoline fumes to the right spot. Concentrated gasoline fumes will force groundhogs, ground squirrels, skunks, and other small animals out of their burrows in a great hurry.

Snakes frequently inhabit the burrows and dens of rodents, and they also come charging out when gasoline fumes becomme intolerable.

HAVAHART TRAPS

The movement toward humane trapping was responsible for the development of the Havahart® Trap. In most communities it is simply impossible to use steel traps. The old box trap gave way to this new wire Havahart® trap, which opens at both ends so the animal entering the trap gets a feeling of confidence that he is going to get out again.

The Havahart® trap is made in standard sizes so you can catch anything from a mouse to a fox.

With these traps it is now possible for the farmer or suburbanite to eliminate pests from his property without harming pets or valuable animals. He can simply transport some of the animals to a place where they can do no harm, and does not have to kill them unless he feels it is desirable.

No. 2 Trap — one end set

3

Planting and Care

What to Grow

Most beginners plant too many different kinds of vegetables without considering what they really expect to harvest. It is far better to begin with the most widely used and easier grown things—such as string beans, tomatoes, beets, lettuce, cucumbers, cabbage, squash, chard, peas, onions, and turnips. Naturally, one can expand, contract, or change these items as desired—I am merely trying to get you to be a practical gardener and plan on lots of string beans and perhaps no cabbage—if you like the beans and do not like cabbage. Plant the things you enjoy eating and plant in sufficient quantities to lower your food bill and last throughout the season.

Where space limitations compel a choice, it is well to consider the value of the yield of a vegetable plant in deciding what to plant. So, in planning the size of your garden, you must decide what you want to grow as well as consider the relative yields and values. In order to get maximum use of your garden plot, you may grow both a crop of

31

early and a crop of late vegetables on the same plot of land. After the peas, early potatoes, and green onions are harvested, one can plant late cabbage, turnips, and kale. These are but a few of the successive plantings that are easy to accomplish. Where a medium-to-long growing season makes such successive plantings possible, a small garden plot can actually be doubled in size with regard to actual yield of vegetables. There are seemingly endless combinations of early, mid-season, and late vegetable crops that may be used for succession planting or intercropping.

Plan your garden with care. Plant pole beans and corn where they will not shade lower plants. It is best to group the tall-growing plants at one end and in rows running east to west to best use the orbit of the sun. Rotation of crops will help keep the soil fertility in balance, inasmuch as different plants take different amounts of nutrients from the soil. Also, bear in mind the grouping of early vegetables so that when harvested, one can till the area and prepare the soil for successive planting of later crops. For example, peas, potatoes, and early cabbage followed by turnips, kale, and beets. One can have a continuous supply of lettuce, beets, and carrots by successive sowings of ten-foot rows of each type at intervals of two or three weeks, depending on rate of growth and use. And, a thirty-foot row need not be reserved for one vegetable—three kinds will grow as readily as one in a row. Radishes may be used to mark the rows of any vegetable—they germinate rapidly, thus marking the row.

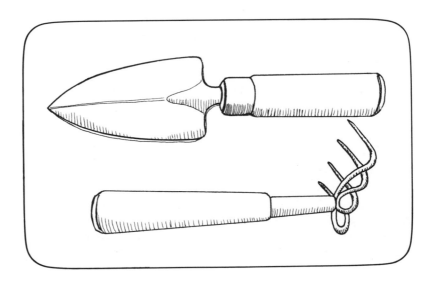

Planted thinly, at intervals of twelve inches, they also provide a bonus wherever used.

On a small plot, it is feasible to grow many vegetables in rows only a foot apart. This includes beets, carrots, leaf lettuce, onions, dwarf peas, radishes, and spinach. Others require more room. Plan on a circle 5 feet in diameter for a hill of squash. A well-planted hill of zucchini will keep pumping out fruits for the table over a period of two to three months. They are vigorous, highly productive, and easily grown. After the vines attain full-growth, they require no further attention other than keeping the fruits picked.

EARLIEST DATES, AND RANGE OF DATES, FOR SAFE SPRING PLANTING OF VEGETABLES IN THE OPEN

Crop	Planting dates for localities in which average date of last freeze is—		
	Jan. 30	Feb. 8	Feb. 18
Asparagus [1]			
Beans, lima	Feb. 1–Apr. 15	Feb. 10–May 1	Mar. 1–May 1
Beans, snap	Feb. 1–Apr. 1	Feb. 1–May 1	Mar. 1–May 1
Beet	Jan. 1–Mar. 15	Jan. 10–Mar. 15	Jan. 20–Apr. 1
Broccoli, sprouting [1]	Jan. 1–30	Jan. 1–30	Jan. 15–Feb. 15
Brussels sprouts [1]	Jan. 1–30	Jan. 1–30	Jan. 15–Feb. 15
Cabbage [1]	Jan. 1–15	Jan. 1–Feb. 10	Jan. 1–Feb. 25
Cabbage, Chinese	[2]	[2]	[2]
Carrot	Jan. 1–Mar. 1	Jan. 1–Mar. 1	Jan. 15–Mar. 1
Cauliflower [1]	Jan. 1–Feb. 1	Jan. 1–Feb. 1	Jan. 10–Feb. 10
Celery and celeriac	Jan. 1–Feb. 1	Jan. 10–Feb. 10	Jan. 20–Feb. 20
Chard	Jan. 1–Apr. 1	Jan. 10–Apr. 1	Jan. 20–Apr. 15
Chervil and chives	Jan. 1–Feb. 1	Jan. 1–Feb. 1	Jan. 1–Feb. 1
Chicory, witloof			
Collards [1]	Jan. 1–Feb. 15	Jan. 1–Feb. 15	Jan. 1–Mar. 15
Cornsalad	Jan. 1–Feb. 15	Jan. 1–Feb. 15	Jan. 1–Mar. 15
Corn, sweet	Feb. 1–Mar. 15	Feb. 10–Apr. 1	Feb. 20–Apr. 15
Cress, upland	Jan. 1–Feb. 1	Jan. 1–Feb. 15	Jan. 15–Feb. 15
Cucumber	Feb. 15–Mar. 15	Feb. 15–Apr. 1	Feb. 15–Apr. 15
Eggplant [1]	Feb. 1–Mar. 1	Feb. 10–Mar. 15	Feb. 20–Apr. 1
Endive	Jan. 1–Mar. 1	Jan. 1–Mar. 1	Jan. 15–Mar. 1
Fennel, Florence	Jan. 1–Mar. 1	Jan. 1–Mar. 1	Jan. 15–Mar. 1
Garlic	[2]	[2]	[2]
Horseradish [1]			
Kale	Jan. 1–Feb. 1	Jan. 10–Feb. 1	Jan. 20–Feb. 10
Kohlrabi	Jan. 1–Feb. 1	Jan. 10–Feb. 1	Jan. 20–Feb. 10
Leek	Jan. 1–Feb. 1	Jan. 1–Feb. 1	Jan. 1–Feb. 15
Lettuce, head [1]	Jan. 1–Feb. 1	Jan. 1–Feb. 1	Jan. 1–Feb. 1
Lettuce, leaf	Jan. 1–Feb. 1	Jan. 1–Feb. 1	Jan. 1–Mar. 15
Muskmelon	Feb. 15–Mar. 15	Feb. 15–Apr. 1	Feb. 15–Apr. 15
Mustard	Jan. 1–Mar. 1	Jan. 1–Mar. 1	Feb. 15–Apr. 15
Okra	Feb. 15–Apr. 1	Feb. 15–Apr. 15	Mar. 1–June 1
Onion [1]	Jan. 1–15	Jan. 1–15	Jan. 1–15
Onion, seed	Jan. 1–15	Jan. 1–15	Jan. 1–15
Onion, sets	Jan. 1–15	Jan. 1–15	Jan. 1–15
Parsley	Jan. 1–30	Jan. 1–30	Jan. 1–30
Parsnip			Jan. 1–Feb. 1
Peas, garden	Jan. 1–Feb. 15	Jan. 1–Feb. 15	Jan. 1–Mar. 1
Peas, black-eye	Feb. 15–May 1	Feb. 15–May 15	Mar. 1–June 15
Pepper [1]	Feb. 1–Apr. 1	Feb. 15–Apr. 15	Mar. 1–May 1
Potato	Jan. 1–Feb. 15	Jan. 1–Feb. 15	Jan. 15–Mar. 1
Radish	Jan. 1–Apr. 1	Jan. 1–Apr. 1	Jan. 1–Apr. 1
Rhubarb [1]			
Rutabaga			
Salsify	Jan. 1–Feb. 1	Jan. 10–Feb. 10	Jan. 15–Feb. 20
Shallot	Jan. 1–Feb. 1	Jan. 1–Feb. 10	Jan. 1–Feb. 20
Sorrel	Jan. 1–Mar. 1	Jan. 1–Mar. 1	Jan. 15–Mar. 1
Soybean	Mar. 1–June 30	Mar. 1–June 30	Mar. 10–June 30
Spinach	Jan. 1–Feb. 15	Jan. 1–Feb. 15	Jan. 1–Mar. 1
Spinach, New Zealand	Feb. 1–Apr. 15	Feb. 15–Apr. 15	Mar. 1–Apr. 15
Squash, summer	Feb. 1–Apr. 15	Feb. 15–Apr. 15	Mar. 1–Apr. 15
Sweetpotato	Feb. 15–May 15	Mar. 1–May 15	Mar. 20–June 1
Tomato	Feb. 1–Apr. 1	Feb. 20–Apr. 10	Mar. 1–Apr. 20
Turnip	Jan. 1–Mar. 1	Jan. 1–Mar. 1	Jan. 10–Mar. 1
Watermelon	Feb. 15–Mar. 15	Feb. 15–Apr. 1	Feb. 15–Apr. 15

[1] Plants.
[2] Generally fall-planted (table 5).

EARLIEST DATES, AND RANGE OF DATES, FOR SAFE SPRING PLANTING OF VEGETABLES IN THE OPEN (CONT.)

Planting dates for localities in which average date of last freeze is—			
Feb. 28	**Mar. 10**	**Mar. 20**	**Mar. 30**
----	Jan. 1-Mar. 1	Feb. 1-Mar. 10	Feb. 15-Mar. 20.
Mar. 15-June 1	Mar. 20-June 1	Apr. 1-June 15	Apr. 15-June 20.
Mar. 10-May 15	Mar. 15-May 15	Mar. 15-May 25	Apr. 1-June 1.
Feb. 1-Apr. 15	Feb. 15-June 1	Feb. 15-May 15	Mar. 1-June 1.
Feb. 1-Mar. 1	Feb. 15-Mar. 15	Feb. 15-Mar. 15	Mar. 1-20.
Feb. 1-Mar. 1	Feb. 15-Mar. 15	Feb. 15-Mar. 15	Mar. 1-20.
Jan. 15-Feb. 25	Jan. 25-Mar. 1	Feb. 1-Mar. 1	Feb. 15-Mar. 10.
(2)	(2)	(2)	(2)
Feb. 1-Mar. 1	Feb. 10-Mar. 15	Feb. 15-Mar. 20	Mar. 1-Apr. 10.
Jan. 20-Feb. 20	Feb. 1-Mar. 1	Feb. 10-Mar. 10	Feb. 20-Mar. 20.
Feb. 1-Mar. 1	Feb. 20-Mar. 20	Mar. 1-Apr. 1	Mar. 15-Apr. 15.
Feb. 1-May 1	Feb. 15-May 15	Feb. 20-May 15	Mar. 1-May 25.
Jan. 15-Feb. 15	Feb. 1-Mar. 1	Feb. 10-Mar. 10	Feb. 15-Mar. 15.
----	June 1-July 1	June 1-July 1	June 1-July 1.
Jan. 15-Mar. 15	Feb. 1-Apr. 1	Feb. 15-May 1	Mar. 1-June 1.
Jan. 1-Mar. 1	Jan. 1-Mar. 15	Jan. 1-Mar. 15	Jan. 15-Mar. 15.
Mar. 1-Apr. 15	Mar. 10-Apr. 15	Mar. 15-May 1	Mar. 25-May 15.
Feb. 1-Mar. 1	Feb. 10-Mar. 15	Feb. 20-Mar. 15	Mar. 1-Apr. 1.
Mar. 1-Apr. 15	Mar. 15-Apr. 15	Apr. 1-May 1	Apr. 10-May 15.
Mar. 10-Apr. 15	Mar. 15-Apr. 15	Apr. 1-May 1	Apr. 15-May 15.
Feb. 1-Mar. 1	Feb. 15-Mar. 15	Mar. 1-Apr. 1	Mar. 10-Apr. 10.
Feb. 1-Mar. 1	Feb. 15-Mar. 15	Mar. 1-Apr. 1	Mar. 10-Apr. 10.
(2)	(2)	Feb. 1-Mar. 1	Feb. 10-Mar. 10.
			Mar. 1-Apr. 1.
Feb. 1-20	Feb. 10-Mar. 1	Feb. 20-Mar. 10	Mar. 1-20.
Feb. 1-20	Feb. 10-Mar. 1	Feb. 20-Mar. 10	Mar. 1-Apr. 1.
Jan. 15-Feb. 15	Jan. 25-Mar. 1	Feb. 1-Mar. 1	Feb. 15-Mar. 15.
Jan. 15-Feb. 15	Feb. 1-20	Feb. 15-Mar. 10	Mar. 1-20.
Jan. 1-Mar. 15	Jan. 15-Apr. 1	Feb. 1-Apr. 1	Feb. 15-Apr. 15.
Mar. 1-Apr. 15	Mar. 1-Apr. 15	Apr. 1-May 1	Apr. 10-May 15.
Feb. 1-Mar. 1	Feb. 10-Mar. 15	Feb. 20-Apr. 1	Mar. 1-Apr. 15.
Mar. 10-June 1	Mar. 20-June 1	Apr. 1-June 15	Apr. 10-June 15.
Jan. 1-Feb. 1	Jan. 15-Feb. 15	Feb. 10-Mar. 10	Feb. 15-Mar. 15.
Jan. 1-Feb. 15	Feb. 1-Mar. 1	Feb. 10-Mar. 10	Feb. 20-Mar. 20.
Jan. 1-Mar. 1	Jan. 15-Mar. 10	Feb. 1-Mar. 20	Feb. 15-Mar. 20.
Jan. 15-Mar. 1	Feb. 1-Mar. 10	Feb. 15-Mar. 15	Mar. 1-Apr. 1.
Jan. 15-Feb. 15	Jan. 15-Mar. 1	Feb. 15-Mar. 15	Mar. 1-Apr. 1.
Jan. 15-Mar. 1	Jan. 15-Mar. 15	Feb. 1-Mar. 15	Feb. 10-Mar. 20.
Mar. 10-June 20	Mar. 15-July 1	Apr. 1-July 1	Apr. 15-July 1.
Mar. 15-May 1	Apr. 1-June 1	Apr. 10-June 1	Apr. 15-June 1.
Jan. 15-Mar. 1	Feb. 1-Mar. 1	Feb. 10-Mar. 15	Feb. 20-Mar. 20.
Jan. 1-Apr. 1	Jan. 1-Apr. 15	Jan. 20-May 1	Feb. 15-May 1.
Jan. 1-Feb. 1	Jan. 15-Feb. 15	Jan. 15-Mar. 1	Feb. 1-Mar. 1.
Jan. 15-Mar. 1	Feb. 1-Mar. 1	Feb. 15-Mar. 1	Mar. 1-15.
Jan. 1-Mar. 1	Jan. 15-Mar. 1	Feb. 1-Mar. 10	Feb. 15-Mar. 15.
Feb. 1-Mar. 10	Feb. 10-Mar. 15	Feb. 10-Mar. 20	Feb. 20-Apr. 1.
Mar. 20-June 30	Apr. 10-June 30	Apr. 10-June 30	Apr. 20-June 30.
Jan. 1-Mar. 1	Jan. 15-Mar. 1	Jan. 15-Mar. 1	Feb. 1-Mar. 20.
Mar. 15-May 15	Mar. 20-May 15	Apr. 1-May 15	Apr. 10-June 1.
Mar. 15-May 15	Mar. 20-May 15	Apr. 1-May 15	Apr. 10-June 1.
Mar. 20-June 1	Apr. 1-June 1	Apr. 10-June 1	Apr. 20-June 1.
Mar. 10-May 1	Mar. 20-May 10	Apr. 1-May 20	Apr. 10-June 1.
Jan. 20-Mar. 1	Feb. 1-Mar. 1	Feb. 10-Mar. 10	Feb. 20-Mar. 20.
Mar. 1-Apr. 15	Mar. 15-Apr. 15	Apr. 1-May 1	Apr. 10-May 15.

EARLIEST DATES, AND RANGE OF DATES, FOR SAFE SPRING PLANTING OF VEGETABLES IN THE OPEN (CONT.)

Crop	Planting dates for localities in which average date of last freeze is—		
	Apr. 10	Apr. 20	Apr. 30
Asparagus [1]	Mar. 10–Apr. 10 ----	Mar. 15–Apr. 15 ----	Mar. 20–Apr. 15 ----
Beans, lima	Apr. 1–June 30 ----	May 1–June 20 ----	May 15–June 15 ----
Beans, snap	Apr. 10–June 30 ---	Apr. 25–June 30 ---	May 10–June 30 ---
Beet	Mar. 10–June 1 ----	Mar. 20–June 1 ----	Apr. 1–June 15 ----
Broccoli, sprouting [1]	Mar. 15–Apr. 15 ----	Mar. 25–Apr. 20 ----	Apr. 1–May 1 ------
Brussels sprouts [1]	Mar. 15–Apr. 15 ----	Mar. 25–Apr. 20 ----	Apr. 1–May 1 ------
Cabbage [1]	Mar. 1–Apr. 1 ------	Mar. 10–Apr. 1 -----	Mar. 15–Apr. 10 ----
Cabbage, Chinese	(²)	(²)	(²)
Carrot	Mar. 10–Apr. 20 ----	Apr. 1–May 15 ------	Apr. 10–June 1 ----
Cauliflower [1]	Mar. 1–Mar. 20 ----	Mar. 15–Apr. 20 ----	Apr. 10–May 10 ----
Celery and celeriac	Apr. 1–Apr. 20 -----	Apr. 10–May 1 -----	Apr. 15–May 1 ----
Chard	Mar. 15–June 15 ---	Apr. 1–June 15 ----	Apr. 15–June 15 ---
Chervil and chives	Mar. 1–Apr. 1 ------	Mar. 10–Apr. 10 ----	Mar. 20–Apr. 20 ----
Chicory, witloof	June 10–July 1 ----	June 15–July 1 ----	June 15–July 1 ----
Collards [1]	Mar. 1–June 1 -----	Mar. 10–June 1 ----	Apr. 1–June 1 -----
Cornsalad	Feb. 1–Apr. 1 -----	Feb. 15–Apr. 15 ----	Mar. 1–May 1 -----
Corn, sweet	Apr. 10–June 1 ----	Apr. 25–June 15 ---	May 10–June 15 ---
Cress, upland	Mar. 10–Apr. 15 ----	Mar. 20–May 1 -----	Apr. 10–May 10 ----
Cucumber	Apr. 20–June 1 ----	May 1–June 15 ----	May 15–June 15 ----
Eggplant [1]	May 1–June 1 -----	May 10–June 1 ----	May 15–June 10 ---
Endive	Mar. 15–Apr. 15 ----	Mar. 25–Apr. 15 ----	Apr. 1–May 1 ------
Fennel, Florence	Mar. 15–Apr. 15 ----	Mar. 25–Apr. 15 ----	Apr. 1–May 1 ------
Garlic	Feb. 20–Mar. 20 ----	Mar. 10–Apr. 1 ----	Mar. 15–Apr. 15 ----
Horseradish [1]	Mar. 10–Apr. 10 ----	Mar. 20–Apr. 20 ----	Apr. 1–30 ---------
Kale	Mar. 10–Apr. 1 ----	Mar. 20–Apr. 10 ----	Apr. 1–20 ---------
Kohlrabi	Mar. 10–Apr. 10 ----	Mar. 20–May 1 -----	Apr. 1–May 10 -----
Leek	Mar. 1–Apr. 1 ------	Mar. 15–Apr. 15 ----	Apr. 1–May 1 -----
Lettuce, head [1]	Mar. 10–Apr. 1 ----	Mar. 20–Apr. 15 ----	Apr. 1–May 1 ------
Lettuce, leaf	Mar. 15–May 15 ----	Mar. 20–May 15 ----	Apr. 1–June 1 -----
Muskmelon	Apr. 20–June 1 ----	May 1–June 15 ----	May 15–June 15 ---
Mustard	Mar. 10–Apr. 20 ----	Mar. 20–May 1 -----	Apr. 1–May 10 -----
Okra	Apr. 20–June 15 ----	May 1–June 1 ------	May 10–June 1 -----
Onion [1]	Mar. 1–Apr. 1 ------	Mar. 15–Apr. 10 ----	Apr. 1–May 1 ------
Onion, seed	Mar. 1–Apr. 1 ------	Mar. 15–Apr. 1 ----	Mar. 15–Apr. 15 ----
Onion, sets	Mar. 1–Apr. 1 ------	Mar. 10–Apr. 1 -----	Mar. 10–Apr. 10 ----
Parsley	Mar. 10–Apr. 10 ----	Mar. 20–Apr. 20 ----	Apr. 1–May 1 ------
Parsnip	Mar. 10–Apr. 10 ----	Mar. 20–Apr. 20 ----	Apr. 1–May 1 ------
Peas, garden	Feb. 20–Mar. 20 ----	Mar. 10–Apr. 10 ----	Mar. 20–May 1 -----
Peas, black-eye	May 1–July 1 -----	May 10–June 15 ---	May 15–June 1 ----
Pepper [1]	May 1–June 1 -----	May 10–June 1 ----	May 15–June 10 ---
Potato	Mar. 10–Apr. 1 ----	Mar. 15–Apr. 10 ----	Mar. 20–May 10 ---
Radish	Mar. 1–May 1 -----	Mar. 10–May 10 ----	Mar. 20–May 10 ---
Rhubarb [1]	Mar. 1–Apr. 1 ------	Mar. 10–Apr. 10 ----	Mar. 20–Apr. 15 ----
Rutabaga	--------------------	--------------------	May 1–June 1 ----
Salsify	Mar. 10–Apr. 15 ----	Mar. 20–May 1 -----	Apr. 1–May 15 -----
Shallot	Mar. 1–Apr. 1 -----	Mar. 15–Apr. 15 ----	Apr. 1–May 1 -----
Sorrel	Mar. 1–Apr. 15 -----	Mar. 15–May 1 -----	Apr. 1–May 15 -----
Soybean	May 1–June 30 ----	May 10–June 20 ---	May 15–June 15 ---
Spinach	Feb. 15–Apr. 1 ----	Mar. 1–Apr. 15 ----	Mar. 20–Apr. 20 ---
Spinach, New Zealand	Apr. 20–June 1 ----	May 1–June 15 ----	May 1–June 15 ----
Squash, summer	Apr. 20–June 1 ----	May 1–June 15 ----	May 1–30 ---------
Sweetpotato	May 1–June 1 ------	May 10–June 10 ---	May 20–June 10 ---
Tomato	Apr. 20–June 1 ----	May 5–June 10 ----	May 10–June 15 ---
Turnip	Mar. 1–Apr. 1 ------	Mar. 10–Apr. 1 -----	Mar. 20–May 1 -----
Watermelon	Apr. 20–June 1 ----	May 1–June 15 ----	May 15–June 15 ---

[1] Plants.
[2] Generally fall-planted (table 5).

EARLIEST DATES, AND RANGE OF DATES, FOR SAFE SPRING PLANTING OF VEGETABLES IN THE OPEN (CONT.)

Planting dates for localities in which average date of last freeze is—			
May 10	May 20	May 30	June 10
Mar. 10–Apr. 30	Apr. 20–May 15	May 1–June 1	May 15–June 1.
May 25–June 15			
May 10–June 30	May–15–June 30	May 25–June 15	
Apr. 15–June 15	Apr. 25–June 15	May 1–June 15	May 15–June 15.
Apr. 15–June 1	May 1–June 15	May 10–June 10	May 20–June 10.
Apr. 15–June 1	May 1–June 15	May 10–June 10	May 20–June 10.
Apr. 1–May 15	May 1–June 15	May 10–June 15	May 20–June 1.
Apr. 1–May 15	May 1–June 15	May 10–June 15	May 20–June 1.
Apr. 20–June 15	May 1–June 1	May 10–June 1	May 20–June 1.
Apr. 15–May 15	May 10–June 15	May 20–June 1	June 1- June 15.
Apr. 20–June 15	May 10–June 15	May 20–June 1	June 1–June 15.
Apr. 20–June 15	May 10–June 15	May 20–June 1	June 1–June 15.
Apr. 1–May 1	Apr. 15–May 15	May 1–June 1	May 15–June 1.
June 1–20	June 1–15	June 1–15	June 1–15.
Apr. 15–June 1	May 1–June 1	May 10–June 1	May 20–June 1.
Apr. 1–June 1	Apr. 15–June 1	May 1–June 15	May 15–June 15.
May 10–June 1	May 15–June 1	May 20–June 1	
Apr. 20–May 20	May 1–June 1	May 15–June 1	May 15–June 15.
May 20–June 15	June 1–15		
May 20–June 15	June 1–15		
Apr. 15–May 15	May 1–30	May 1–30	May 15–June 1.
Apr. 15–May 15	May 1–30	May 1–30	May 15–June 1.
Apr. 1–May 1	Apr. 15–May 15	May 1–30	May 15–June 1.
Apr. 15–May 15	Apr. 20–May 20	May 1–30	May 15–June 1.
Apr. 10–May 1	Apr. 20–May 10	May 1–30	May 15–June 1.
Apr. 10–May 15	Apr. 20–May 20	May 1–30	May 15–June 1.
Apr. 15–May 15	May 1–May 20	May 1–15	May 1–15.
Apr. 15–May 15	May 1–June 30	May 10–June 30	May 20–June 30.
Apr. 15–June 15	May 1–June 30	May 10–June 30	May 20–June 30.
June 1–June 15			
Apr. 15–June 1	May 1–June 30	May 10–June 30	May 20–June 30.
May 20–June 10	June 1–20		
Apr. 10–May 1	Apr. 20–May 15	May 1–30	May 10–June 10.
Apr. 1–May 1	Apr. 20–May 15	May 1–30	May 10–June 10.
Apr. 10–May 1	Apr. 20–May 15	May 1–30	May 10–June 10.
Apr. 15–May 15	May 1–20	May 10–June 1	May 20–June 10.
Apr. 15- May 15	May 1–20	May 10–June 1	May 20–June 10.
Apr. 1–May 15	Apr. 15–June 1	May 1–June 15	May 10–June 15.
May 20–June 10	May 25–June 15	June 1–15	
Apr. 1–June 1	Apr. 15–June 15	May 1–June 15	May 15–June 1.
Apr. 1–June 1	Apr. 15–June 15	May 1–June 15	May 15–June 1.
Apr. 1–May 1	Apr. 15–May 10	May 1–20	May 15–June 1.
May 1–June 1	May 1–20	May 10–20	May 20–June 1.
Apr. 15–June 1	May 1–June 1	May 10–June 1	May 20–June 1.
Apr. 10–May 1	Apr. 20–May 10	May 1–June 1	May 10–June 1.
Apr. 15–June 1	May 1–June 1	May 10–June 10	May 20–June 10.
May 25–June 10			
Apr. 1–June 15	Apr. 10–June 15	Apr. 20–June 15	May 1–June 15.
May 10–June 15	May 20–June 15	June 1–15	
May 10–June 10	May 20–June 15	June 1–20	June 10–20.
May 15–June 10	May 25–June 15	June 5–20	June 15–30.
Apr. 1–June 1	Apr. 15–June 1	May 1–June 15	May 15–June 15.
June 1–June 15	June 15–July 1		

SOME COMMON VEGETABLES
GROUPED ACCORDING TO THE APPROXIMATE
TIMES THEY CAN BE PLANTED AND THEIR RELATIVE
REQUIREMENTS FOR COOL AND WARM WEATHER

Cold-hardy plants for early-spring planting		Cold-tender or heat-hardy plants for later-spring or early-summer planting			Hardy plants for late-summer or fall planting except in the North (plant 6 to 8 weeks before first fall freeze)
Very hardy (plant 4 to 6 weeks before frost-free date)	Hardy (plant 2 to 4 weeks before frost-free date)	Not cold-hardy (plant on frost-free date)	Requiring hot weather (plant 1 week or more after frost-free date)	Medium heat-tolerant (good for summer planting)	
Broccoli	Beets	Beans, snap	Beans, lima	Beans, all	Beets
Cabbage	Carrot	Okra	Eggplant	Chard	Collard
Lettuce	Chard	New Zea-	Peppers	Soybean	Kale
Onions	Mustard	land	Sweetpo-	New Zea-	Lettuce
Peas	Parsnip	spinach	tato	land	Mustard
Potato	Radish	Soybean	Cucum-	spinach	Spinach
Spinach		Squash	ber	Squash	Turnip
Turnip		Sweet corn	Melons	Sweet	
		Tomato		corn	

When to Plant

The time for planting or transplanting is very important—both from the standpoint of vigorous, productive plants and that of their mere survival. For example, eggplants that are set outdoors before the ground is warm and daily temperatures are high simply will not grow and thrive. Conversely, peas that are planted too late in the spring to mature before summer heat and high temperatures prevail will not be productive. So, we must time our planting to coincide with the temperature requirements of the various vegetables. Knowing this, we can group them according to their relative hardiness or resistance to cold.

The extremely cold-hardy plants include turnips, potatoes, lettuce, onions, peas, and cabbage. All of these may be planted as early in the spring as the ground can be worked and a month to six weeks before the frost-free date.

The cold-hardy plants include beets, radishes, chard, carrots, and parsnips. All of these should be planted from two to four weeks before the frost-free date.

Those vegetables to be planted after the last killing frost and when temperatures begin to rise, both day and night, include snap beans, squash, New Zealand spinach, tomatoes, and sweet corn.

The truly heat-hardy plants that thrive only on hot weather include lima beans, eggplant, peppers, sweet potatoes, and cucumbers. These are all best planted about two weeks or more after the frost-free date.

The cold-hardy plants that thrive in the fall include kale, beets, mustard, turnips, late cabbage, and lettuce. Planting must be made in late summer in time to allow for maturity before the first freeze, except for turnips and kale. Both of these thrive on repeated frosts.

LATEST DATES, AND RANGE OF DATES, FOR SAFE FALL PLANTING OF VEGETABLES IN THE OPEN

Crop	Planting dates for localities in which average dates of first freeze is—					
	Aug. 30	Sept. 10	Sept. 20	Sept. 30	Oct. 10	Oct. 20
Asparagus[1]					Oct. 20–Nov. 15 -	Nov. 1–Dec. 15.
Beans, lima				June 1–15 ----	June 1–15 ----	June 15–30.
Beans, snap		May 15–June 15 -	June 1–July 1 -	June 1–July 10 --	June 15–July 20 -	July 1–Aug. 1.
Beet	May 15–June 15 -	May 15–June 15 -	June 1–July 1 -	June 1–July 10 --	June 15–July 25 -	July 1–Aug. 5.
Broccoli, sprouting	May 1–June 1 -	May 1–June 1 ---	May 1–June 15 --	June 1–30 ----	June 15–July 15 -	July 1–Aug. 1.
Brussels sprouts	May 1–June 1 ---	May 1–June 1 ---	May 1–June 15 --	June 1–30 -----	June 15–July 15 -	July 1–Aug. 1.
Cabbage[1]	May 1–June 1 -	May 1–June 1 ---	May 1–June 15 --	June 1–July 10 --	June 1–July 15 --	July 1–20.
Cabbage, Chinese	May 15–June 15 -	May 15–June 15 -	June 1–July 1 -	June 1–July 15 --	June 15–Aug. 1 -	July 15–Aug. 15.
Carrot	May 15–June 15 -	May 15–June 15 -	June 1–July 1 --	June 1–July 10 --	June 1–July 20 --	June 15–Aug. 1.
Cauliflower[1]	May 1–June 1 ---	May 1–July 1 ---	May 1–July 1 ---	May 10–July 15 -	June 1–July 25 --	July 1–Aug. 5.
Celery[1] and celeriac	May 1–June 1 -	May 15–June 15 -	May 15–July 1 --	June 1–July 5 --	June 1–July 15 --	June 1–Aug. 1.
Chard	May 15–June 15 -	May 15–July 1 -	June 1–July 1 --	June 1–July 5 --	June 1–July 20 --	June 1–Aug. 1.
Chervil and chives	May 10–June 10 -	May 1–June 15 -	May 15–June 15 -	(²)	(²)	(²)
Chicory, witloof	May 15–June 15 -	May 15–June 15 -	May 15–June 15 -	June 1–July 1 --	June 1–July 1 ---	June 15–July 15.
Collards[1]	May 15–June 15 -	May 15–June 15 -	May 15–June 15 -	June 15–July 15 -	July 1–Aug. 1 --	July 15–Aug. 15.
Cornsalad	May 15–June 15 -	May 15–July 1 --	June 15–Aug. 1 -	July 15–Sept. 1 -	Aug. 15–Sept. 15	Sept. 1–Oct. 15.
Corn, sweet			June 1–July 1 ---	June 1–July 1 --	June 1–July 10 --	June 1–July 20.
Cress, upland	May 15–June 15 -	May 15–July 1 ---	June 15–Aug. 1 -	July 15–Sept. 1 --	Aug. 15–Sept. 15	Sept. 1–Oct. 15.
Cucumber			June 1–15 ---	June 1–July 1 --	June 1–July 1 --	June 1–July 15.
Eggplant[1]				May 20–June 10 -	May 15–June 15 -	June 1–July 1.
Endive	June 1–July 1 ---	June 1–July 1 ---	June 15–July 15 -	June 15–Aug. 1 --	July 1–Aug. 15 -	July 15–Sept. 1.
Fennel, Florence	May 15–June 15 -	May 15–July 15 -	June 1–July 1 --	June 1–July 1 ---	June 15–July 15 -	June 15–Aug. 1.
Garlic	(²)	(²)	(²)	(²)	(²)	(²)
Horseradish[1]	(²)	(²)	(²)	(²)	(²)	(²)
Kale	May 15–June 15 -	May 15–June 15 -	June 1–July 1 ---	June 15–July 15 -	July 1–Aug. 1 -	July 15–Aug. 15.

Crop						
Kohlrabi	May 15–June 15	June 1–July 1	June 1–July 15	June 15–July 15	July 1–Aug. 1	July 15–Aug. 15.
Leek	May 1–June 1	May 1–July 1	(2)	(2)	(2)	(2)
Lettuce, head [1]	May 15–July 1	May 15–July 1	June 1–July 15	June 15–Aug. 1	July 15–Aug. 15	Aug. 1–30.
Lettuce, leaf	May 15–July 15	May 15–July 15	June 1–Aug. 1	June 1–Aug. 1	July 15–Sept. 1	July 15–Sept. 1.
Muskmelon	May 15–July 15	May 15–July 15	May 15–June 15	May 15–June 15	June 1–June 15	June 15–July 20.
Mustard	May 15–July 15	May 1–June 10	June 1–July 1	June 15–Aug. 1	July 15–Aug. 15	Aug. 1–Sept. 1.
Okra	May 1–June 10	May 1–June 1	June 1–20	June 1–July 1	June 1–July 15	June 1–Aug. 1.
Onion [1]	May 1–June 1	June 1–20	(2)	(2)	(2)	(2)
Onion, seed	May 1–June 10	(2)	(2)	(2)	(2)	(2)
Onion, sets	May 1–June 10	(2)	(2)	(2)	(2)	(2)
Parsley	May 15–June 15	May 1–June 15	June 1–July 1	June 1–July 15	June 15–Aug. 1	July 15–Aug. 15.
Parsnip [1]	May 15–June 1	May 1–June 15	May 15–June 15	June 1–July 1	June 1–July 10	(2)
Peas, garden	May 10–June 15	May 1–July 1	June 1–July 15	June 1–Aug. 1	(2)	(2)
Peas, black-eye		June 1–June 20	June 1–July 1	June 1–July 1	June 1–July 1	June 1–July 1.
Pepper [1]	May 1–June 1	May 1–June 15	June 1–20	May 1–June 15	June 1–July 1	June 1–July 10.
Potato	May 15–June 1	May 1–Aug. 1	May 1–June 15	May 1–June 15	May 15–June 15	June 15–July 15.
Radish	May 1–July 15	Sept. 1–Oct. 15	Sept. 15–Oct. 15	Aug. 15–Oct. 1	July 15–Sept. 15	Oct. 1.
Rhubarb [1]	Sept. 1–Oct. 1	May 1–June 15	Sept. 15–Nov. 1	Oct. 1–Nov. 1	Oct. 15–Nov. 15	Oct. 15–Dec. 1.
Rutabaga	May 15–June 15	May 10–June 10	June 1–July 1	June 15–Sept. 1	June 15–July 15	July 10–20.
Salsify	May 15–June 1	May 1–June 15	June 1–July 1	June 1–July 1	June 1–July 1	June 1–July 1.
Shallot	(2)	(2)	May 20–June 20	May 20–June 20	May 20–June 10	June 1–July 1.
Sorrel	May 15–June 15	May 1–June 15	June 1–July 1	(2)	(2)	(2)
Soybean	May 15–June 15	May 15–July 1	June 1–July 15	June 1–July 15	July 1–Aug. 1	July 15–Aug. 15.
Spinach	May 15–July 15	June 1–July 15	June 1–Aug. 1	May 25–June 10	June 1–25	June 1–July 5.
Spinach, New Zealand	June 1–July 15	June 1–Aug. 1	June 1–Aug. 15	July 1–Aug. 15	Aug. 1–Sept. 1	Aug. 20–Sept. 10.
Squash, summer	June 1–20	June 1–July 1	May 15–July 1	May 15–July 1	June 1–July 15	June 1–Aug. 1.
Squash, winter	June 1–20	May 15–July 1	May 20–June 10	June 1–July 1	June 1–July 15	June 1–July 20.
Sweetpotato		May 20–June 10	June 1–15	June 1–July 1	June 1–July 1	June 1–July 1.
Tomato	June 20–30	June 1–20	June 1–20	May 20–June 10	May 20–June 10	June 1–15.
Turnip	May 15–June 15	June 1–20	June 1–July 15	June 1–20	June 1–20	June 1–July 1.
Watermelon	May 15–June 15	June 1–July 15	May 15–June 15	July 1–Aug. 1	July 1–Aug. 1	July 15–Aug. 15.
			May 1–June 15	May 15–June 1	May 15–June 15	June 15–July 20.

[1] Plants.

[2] Generally spring-planted (table 4).

41

LATEST DATES, AND RANGE OF DATES, FOR SAFE FALL PLANTING OF VEGETABLES IN THE OPEN (CONT)

Crop	Planting dates for localities in which average date of first freeze is—					
	Oct. 30	Nov. 10	Nov. 20	Nov. 30	Dec. 10	Dec. 20
Asparagus [1]	Nov. 15–Jan. 1	Dec. 1–Jan. 1			Sept. 1–30	Sept. 1–Oct. 1.
Beans, lima	July 1–Aug. 1	July 1–Aug. 15	July 15–Sept. 1	Aug. 1–Sept. 15	Sept. 1–30	Sept. 1–Nov. 1.
Beans, snap	July 1–Aug. 15	July 1–Sept. 1	July 1–Sept. 10	Aug. 15–Sept. 20	Sept. 1–Dec. 31	Sept. 1–Dec. 31.
Beet	Aug. 1–Sept. 1	Aug. 1–Oct. 1	Sept. 1–Dec. 1	Sept. 1–Dec. 15	Aug. 1–Nov. 1	Sept. 1–Dec. 31.
Broccoli, sprouting	July 1–Aug. 15	Aug. 1–Sept. 1	Aug. 1–Sept. 15	Aug. 1–Oct. 1	Aug. 1–Nov. 1	Sept. 1–Dec. 31.
Brussels sprouts	July 1–Aug. 15	Aug. 1–Sept. 1	Aug. 1–Sept. 15	Aug. 1–Oct. 1	Sept. 1–Dec. 31	Sept. 1–Dec. 31.
Cabbage [1]	Aug. 1–Sept. 1	Sept. 1–15	Sept. 1–Dec. 1	Sept. 1–Dec. 31	Sept. 1–Nov. 15	Sept. 1–Dec. 1.
Cabbage, Chinese	Aug. 1–Sept. 15	Aug. 15–Oct. 1	Sept. 1–Oct. 15	Sept. 1–Nov. 1	Sept. 15–Dec. 1	Sept. 15–Dec. 1.
Carrot	July 1–Aug. 15	Aug. 1–Sept. 1	Sept. 1–Nov. 1	Sept. 15–Dec. 1	Sept. 1–Oct. 20	Sept. 15–Nov. 1.
Cauliflower [1]	July 15–Aug. 15	Aug. 1–Sept. 1	Aug. 1–Sept. 15	Aug. 15–Oct. 10	Sept. 1–Dec. 31	Oct. 1–Dec. 31.
Celery [1] and celeriac	June 15–Aug. 15	July 1–Aug. 15	July 15–Sept. 1	Aug. 1–Dec. 1	June 1–Dec. 1	June 1–Dec. 31.
Chard	June 1–Sept. 10	June 1–Sept. 15	June 1–Oct. 1	June 1–Nov. 1	Nov. 1–Dec. 31	Nov. 1–Dec. 31.
Chervil and chives	(2)	(2)	Nov. 1–Dec. 31	Nov. 1–Dec. 31	Aug. 15–Oct. 15	Aug. 15–Oct. 15.
Chicory, witloof	July 1–Aug. 10	July 10–Aug. 20	July 20–Sept. 1	Aug. 15–Sept. 30	Sept. 1–Dec. 31	Sept. 1–Dec. 31.
Collards [1]	Aug. 1–Sept. 15	Aug. 15–Oct. 1	Aug. 25–Nov. 1	Sept. 1–Dec. 1	Oct. 1–Dec. 31	Oct. 1–Dec. 31.
Cornsalad	Sept. 15–Nov. 1	Oct. 1–Dec. 1	Oct. 1–Dec. 1	Oct. 1–Dec. 31	Oct. 1–Dec. 31	
Corn, sweet	June 1–Aug. 1	June 1–Aug. 15	June 1–Sept. 1			
Cress, upland	Sept. 15–Nov. 1	Oct. 1–Dec. 1	Oct. 1–Dec. 1	Oct. 1–Dec. 31	Oct. 1–Dec. 31	Oct. 1–Dec. 31.
Cucumber	June 1–Aug. 1	June 1–Aug. 15	June 1–Aug. 15	July 15–Sept. 15	Aug. 15–Oct. 1	Aug. 15–Oct. 1.
Eggplant [1]	June 1–July 1	June 1–July 15	June 1–Aug. 1	July 1–Sept. 1	Aug. 1–Sept. 30	Aug. 1–Sept. 30.
Endive	July 15–Aug. 15	Aug. 1–Sept. 1	Sept. 1–Oct. 1	Sept. 1–Nov. 15	Sept. 1–Dec. 31	Sept. 1–Dec. 31.
Fennel, Florence	July 1–Aug. 1	July 15–Aug. 15	Aug. 15–Sept. 15	Sept. 1–Nov. 15	Sept. 1–Dec. 1	Sept. 1–Dec. 1.
Garlic	(2)	(2)	(2)	(2)	Sept. 15–Nov. 15	Sept. 15–Nov. 15.
Horseradish [1]	(2)	(2)	(2)	(2)	(2)	(2)
Kale	July 15–Sept. 1	Aug. 1–Sept. 15	Aug. 15–Oct. 15	Sept. 1–Dec. 1	Sept. 1–Dec. 31	Sept. 1–Dec. 31.

Crop						
Kohlrabi	Aug. 1–Sept. 1	Aug. 15–Sept. 15	Sept. 1–Oct. 15	Sept. 1–Dec. 1	Sept. 15–Dec. 31	Sept. 1–Dec. 31
Leek [1]	(2)	(2)	Sept. 1–Nov. 1	Sept. 1–Nov. 1	Sept. 1–Nov. 1	Sept. 15–Nov. 1
Lettuce, head [1]	Aug. 1–Sept. 15	Aug. 15–Oct. 15	Sept. 1–Nov. 1	Sept. 1–Dec. 1	Sept. 15–Dec. 31	Sept. 15–Dec. 31
Lettuce, leaf	Aug. 15–Oct. 1	Aug. 25–Oct. 1	Sept. 1–Nov. 1	Sept. 1–Dec. 1	Sept. 15–Dec. 31	Sept. 15–Dec. 31
Muskmelon	July 1–July 15	July 15–July 30				
Mustard	Aug. 15–Oct. 15	Aug. 15–Nov. 1	Sept. 1–Dec. 1	Sept. 1–Dec. 1	Sept. 1–Dec. 1	Sept. 15–Dec. 1
Okra	June 1–Aug. 10	June 1–Aug. 20	June 1–Sept. 10	June 1–Sept. 20	Aug. 1–Oct. 1	Aug. 1–Oct. 1
Onion [1]		Sept. 1–Oct. 15	Oct. 1–Dec. 31	Oct. 1–Dec. 31	Oct. 1–Dec. 31	Oct. 1–Dec. 31
Onion, seed			Sept. 1–Nov. 1	Sept. 1–Nov. 1	Sept. 1–Nov. 1	Sept. 15–Nov. 1
Onion, sets		Oct. 1–Dec. 1	Nov. 1–Dec. 31	Nov. 1–Dec. 31	Nov. 1–Dec. 31	Nov. 1–Dec. 31
Parsley	Aug. 1–Sept. 15	Sept. 1–Nov. 15	Sept. 1–Dec. 31	Sept. 1–Dec. 31	Sept. 1–Dec. 31	Sept. 1–Dec. 31
Parsnip	(2)	(2)	Aug. 1–Sept. 1	Sept. 1–Nov. 15	Sept. 1–Dec. 1	Sept. 1–Dec. 1
Peas, garden	Aug. 1–Sept. 15	Sept. 1–Nov. 1	Oct. 1–Dec. 1	Oct. 1–Dec. 31	Oct. 1–Dec. 31	Oct. 1–Dec. 1
Peas, black-eye [1]	June 1–Aug. 1	June 15–Aug. 15	July 1–Sept. 1	July 1–Sept. 10	July 1–Sept. 20	July 1–Sept. 20
Pepper [1]	June 1–July 20	June 1–Aug. 1	June 1–Aug. 15	June 15–Sept. 1	Aug. 15–Oct. 1	Aug. 15–Oct. 1
Potato	July 20–Aug. 10	July 25–Aug. 20	Aug. 10–Sept. 15	Aug. 1–Sept. 15	Aug. 1–Sept. 15	Aug. 1–Sept. 15
Radish	Aug. 15–Oct. 15	Sept. 1–Nov. 1	Sept. 1–Dec. 1	Sept. 1–Dec. 31	Aug. 1–Sept. 15	Oct. 1–Dec. 31
Rhubarb [1]	Nov. 1–Dec. 1					
Rutabaga	July 15–Aug. 1	July 15–Aug. 15	Aug. 1–Sept. 1	Sept. 1–Nov. 15	Oct. 1–Nov. 15	Oct. 15–Nov. 15
Salsify	June 1–July 10	June 15–July 20	July 15–Aug. 15	Aug. 15–Sept. 30	Sept. 1–Oct. 15	Sept. 1–Oct. 31
Shallot	(2)	Aug. 1–Oct. 1	Aug. 15–Oct. 1	Aug. 15–Oct. 15	Sept. 1–Dec. 15	Sept. 15–Nov. 1
Sorrel	Aug. 1–Sept. 15	Aug. 15–Oct. 1	Aug. 15–Oct. 15	Sept. 1–Nov. 15	Sept. 1–Dec. 15	Sept. 1–Dec. 31
Soybean	June 1–July 15	June 1–July 25	June 1–July 30	June 1–July 30	June 1–July 30	June 1–July 30
Spinach	Sept. 1–Oct. 1	Sept. 15–Nov. 1	Oct. 1–Dec. 1	Oct. 1–Dec. 31	Oct. 1–Dec. 31	Oct. 1–Dec. 31
Spinach, New Zealand	June 1–Aug. 1	June 1–Aug. 15	June 1–Aug. 15	June 1–Aug. 15		
Squash, summer	June 1–Aug. 1	June 1–Aug. 10	June 1–Aug. 20	June 1–Sept. 1	June 1–Sept. 15	June 1–Oct. 1
Squash, winter	June 10–July 10	June 20–July 20	July 1–Aug. 1	July 15–Aug. 15	Aug. 1–Sept. 1	Aug. 1–Sept. 1
Sweetpotato	June 1–15	June 1–July 1	June 1–July 1	June 1–July 1	June 1–July 1	June 1–July 1
Tomato	June 1–July 1	June 1–July 15	June 1–Aug. 1	Aug. 1–Sept. 1	Aug. 15–Oct. 1	Sept. 1–Nov. 1
Turnip	Aug. 1–Sept. 15	Sept. 1–Oct. 15	Sept. 1–Nov. 15	Sept. 1–Nov. 15	Sept. 1–Nov. 1	Oct. 1–Dec. 31
Watermelon	July 1–July 15	July 15–July 30				

[1] Plants.
[2] Generally spring-planted (table 4).

43

QUANTITY OF SEED AND NUMBER OF PLANTS REQUIRED FOR 100 FEET OF ROW, DEPTHS OF PLANTING, AND DISTANCES APART FOR ROWS AND PLANTS

Crop	Requirement for 100 feet of row		Depth for planting seed	Distance apart		Plants in the row
	Seed	Plants		Rows		
				Horse- or tractor-cultivated	Hand-cultivated	
			Inches	Feet		
Asparagus	1 ounce	75	1 -1½	4 -5	1½ to 2 feet	18 inches.
Beans:						
Lima, bush	½ pound		1 -1½	2½-3	2 feet	3 to 4 inches.
Lima, pole	½ pound		1 -1½	3 -4	3 feet	3 to 4 feet.
Snap, bush	½ pound		1 -1½	2½-3	2 feet	3 to 4 inches.
Snap, pole	4 ounces		1 -1½	3 -4	2 feet	3 feet.
Beet	2 ounces		1	2 -2½	14 to 16 inches	2 to 3 inches.
Broccoli:						
Heading	1 packet	50- 75	½	2½-3	2 to 2½ feet	14 to 24 inches.
Sprouting	1 packet	50- 75	½	2½-3	2 to 2½ feet	14 to 24 inches.
Brussels sprouts	1 packet	50- 75	½	2½-3	2 to 2½ feet	14 to 24 inches.
Cabbage	1 packet	50- 75	½	2½-3	2 to 2½ feet	14 to 24 inches.
Cabbage, Chinese	1 packet		½	2 -2½	18 to 24 inches	8 to 12 inches.
Carrot	1 packet	50- 75	½	2 -2½	14 to 16 inches	2 to 3 inches.
Cauliflower	1 packet	200-250	½	2½-3	2 to 2½ feet	14 to 24 inches.
Celeriac	1 packet	200-250	⅛	2½-3	18 to 24 inches	4 to 6 inches.
Celery	1 packet	200-250	⅛	2½-3	18 to 24 inches	4 to 6 inches.
Chard	2 ounces		1	2 -2½	18 to 24 inches	6 inches.
Chervil	1 packet		½	2 -2½	14 to 16 inches	2 to 3 inches.
Chicory, witloof	1 packet		½	2 -2½	18 to 24 inches	6 to 8 inches.
Chives	1 packet		½	2½-3	14 to 16 inches	In clusters.
Collards	1 packet		½	3 -3½	18 to 24 inches	18 to 24 inches.
Cornsalad	1 packet		½	2½-3	14 to 16 inches	1 foot.
Corn, sweet	2 ounces		2	3 -3½	2 to 3 feet	Drills, 14 to 16 inches; hills, 2½ to 3 feet.
Cress Upland	1 packet		⅛- ¼	2 -2½	14 to 16 inches	2 to 3 inches.
Cucumber	1 packet		½	6 -7	6 to 7 feet	Drills, 3 feet; hills, 6 feet.
Dasheen	5 to 6 pounds		2 -3	3½-4	3½ to 4 feet	2 feet.
Eggplant	1 packet	50	½	3	2 to 2½ feet	3 feet.

44

Endive	1 packet		½	2½–3	18 to 24 inches	12 inches.
Fennel, Florence	1 packet		½	2½–3	18 to 24 inches	4 to 6 inches.
Garlic	1 pound		1 –2	2½–3	14 to 16 inches	2 to 3 inches.
Horseradish	Cuttings	50–75	2	3 –4	2 to 2½ feet	18 to 24 inches.
Kale	1 packet		½	2½–3	18 to 24 inches	12 to 15 inches.
Kohlrabi	1 packet		½	2½–3	14 to 16 inches	5 to 6 inches.
Leek	1 packet		½–1	2½–3	14 to 16 inches	2 to 3 inches.
Lettuce, head	1 packet	100	½	2½–3	14 to 16 inches	12 to 15 inches.
Lettuce, leaf	1 packet		½	2½–3	14 to 16 inches	6 inches.
Muskmelon	1 packet		1	6 –7	6 to 7 feet	Hills, 6 feet.
Mustard	1 packet		½	2½–3	14 to 16 inches	12 inches.
Okra	2 ounces		1 –1½	3 –3½	3 to 3½ feet	2 feet.
Onion:						
Plants		400	1 –2	2 –2½	14 to 16 inches	2 to 3 inches.
Seed	1 packet		½–1	2 –2½	14 to 16 inches	2 to 3 inches.
Sets	1 pound		1 –2	2 –2½	14 to 16 inches	2 to 3 inches.
Parsley	1 packet		⅛	2 –2½	14 to 16 inches	4 to 6 inches.
Parsley, turnip-rooted	1 packet		⅛– ¼	2 –2½	14 to 16 inches	2 to 3 inches.
Parsnip	1 packet		½	2 –2½	18 to 24 inches	2 to 3 inches.
Peas	½ pound		2 –3	2 –4	1½ to 3 feet	1 inch.
Pepper	1 packet	50–70	½	3 –4	2 to 3 feet	18 to 24 inches.
Physalis	1 packet		½	2 –2½	1½ to 2 feet	12 to 18 inches.
Potato	5 to 6 pounds, tubers		4	2½–3	2 to 2½ feet	10 to 18 inches.
Pumpkin	1 ounce		1 –2	5 –8	5 to 8 feet	3 to 4 feet.
Radish	1 ounce		½	2 –2½	14 to 16 inches	1 inch.
Rhubarb		25–35		3 –4	3 to 4 feet	3 to 4 feet.
Salsify	1 ounce		½	2 –2½	18 to 26 inches	2 to 3 inches.
Shallots	1 pound (cloves)		1 –2	2 –2½	12 to 18 inches	2 to 3 inches.
Sorrel	1 packet		½	2 –2½	18 to 24 inches	5 to 8 inches.
Soybean	½ to 1 pound		1 –1½	2½–3	24 to 30 inches	3 inches.
Spinach	1 ounce		½	2 –2½	14 to 16 inches	3 to 4 inches.
Spinach, New Zealand	1 ounce		1 –1½	3 –3½	3 feet	18 inches.
Squash:						
Bush	½ ounce		1 –2	4 –5	4 to 5 feet	Drills, 15 to 18 inches; hills, 4 feet.
Vine	1 ounce		1 –2	8 –12	8 to 12 feet	Drills, 2 to 3 feet; hills, 4 feet.
Sweetpotato	5 pounds, bedroots	75	2 –3	3 –3½	3 to 3½ feet	12 to 14 inches.
Tomato	1 packet	35–50	½	3 –4	2 to 3 feet	1½ to 3 feet.
Turnip greens	1 packet		¼– ½	2 –2½	14 to 16 inches	2 to 3 inches.
Turnips and rutabagas	½ ounce		¼– ½	2 –2½	14 to 16 inches	2 to 3 inches.
Watermelon	1 ounce		1 –2	8 –10	8 to 10 feet	Drills, 2 to 3 feet; hills, 8 feet.

Average dates of the last killing frost in spring.

46

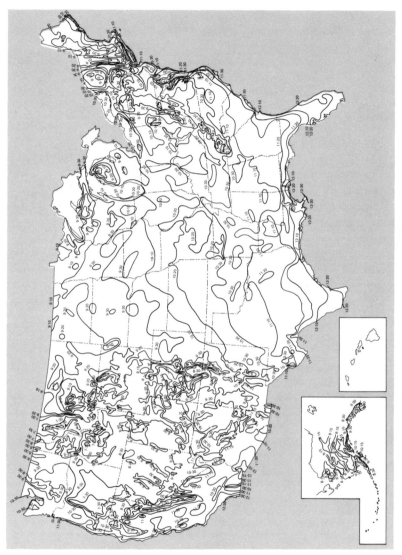

Average dates of the first killing frost in fall.

47

Selecting Seeds

The success of your minigarden or regular garden will depend a great deal on the quality of seed you plant. Here is your chance to be selective. There are many strains and varieties of seeds for each vegetable. Accordingly, select disease- and insect- resistant varieties if they are available. Remember that hybrids are more vigorous and usually more productive, with more uniform yields, over a longer season, than standard varieties, and they are therefore preferable.

Your county agricultural agent or state experimental station will recommend varieties best adapted to your area if you feel that you cannot decide for yourself. This service is free and they will be glad to assist you.

Seeds may be ordered through the mail order seed catalogue or they may be purchased from a local garden supply store or a reputable dealer. Make sure that your packet of seeds has a stamp on it verifying the year that the seeds were packed. Seeds that have remained on shelves in tiny outlets for long periods of time may not germinate properly and may not be of top quality. The average viability of some typical garden seeds and the average percentage of germination under ordinary conditions are as follows:

Kind of Seed	Average Viability in Years	Percentage
Bean	3	80-85
Beet	6	70-75
Cabbage	5	80-85
Carrot	4	70-75
Cucumber	10	80-85
Eggplant	5	60-65
Lettuce	5	70-75
Parsley	3	50-60
Peas	3	80-85
Pepper	4	55-60
Radish	6	85-90
Spinach, New Zealand	5	75-80

Kind of Seed	Average Viability in Years	Percentage
Sweet Corn	2	75-80
Tomato	5	70-75
Turnip	5	75-80

Starting the Plants

Nothing is more interesting than growing plants from tiny seeds for transplanting. This is the fastest, least expensive, and invariably the only way to get the specific varieties that you want. There are no restrictions on the containers to be used for starting seeds. You may use cut-off milk cartons (removing a side panel is a better method), coffee cans, plastic food trays, aluminum foil baking pans (all with drainage holes in the bottom); or you can buy peat trays, clay pots, and molded or fiber trays designed for the purpose. Look in garden supply centers and mail order seed catalogs for additional ideas for starting seeds.

If you use new clay pots it will be necessary to soak them for a few hours in water in order to fill the porous walls with moisture. This prevents excessive loss of soil moisture on initial use. Cover the drainage hole in the bottom of pot with pieces from a broken pot, small pieces of brick, or small stones.

DAMPING-OFF

The principal enemy of indoor plant culture is *damping-off,* which is a disease that makes young seedlings fall over and die. It is a stem rot caused by a fungus that flourishes where there is too much moisture and too little circulation of air. This condition is also encouraged by having seedlings too thick. To get around this hazard we need a sterile medium for the seedbed. This is obtained by using vermiculite, perlite, and sphagnum moss. All of these sterile mediums may be used separately or in any mixture you desire. Equal parts of all three make an excellent seedbed. Potting soil is also a very good medium for starting seed.

THE ACTUAL PLANTING

Fill the planting containers to within a half inch of the top and thump the containers on the table or floor to settle and slightly firm the seed starting medium. Add more of the mixture if it is needed, to bring the level up to a half inch below the top of the container.

One-half-inch furrows made with a jig.

Clear plastic film gives a flat, even, subdued light and holds the moisture.

Very fine seeds, like tomato and pepper, should be sprinkled on top of the seedbed and then firmed in with the flat of the hand or the bottom of a glass, firmly but gently. The standard method is to plant tiny, fine seeds to a depth of two or three times their diameter. For tiny seeds, this depth will amount to approximately 1/16 of an inch; and under no circumstances more than 1/8 inch. Look at this measurement on a ruler in order to fix in your mind the shallowness of such planting. Seeds should be spaced approximately one inch apart. Place a few seeds on a creased piece of stiff paper and gently shake them onto the seedbed. It is a very easy matter to cover the seeds to the desired depth with sphagnum moss that has either been milled or run through a sieve. This use of sphagnum moss is also a good way to prevent damping-off. It is advisable to use a separate pot or flat for each kind of seed; labeling or marking them will enable you to keep track of your project.

WATERING

Set a newly seeded pot or flat in a tub or basin of tepid water and let it remain there until water glistens on the surface of the planting medium. Adequate watering for germination has now been attained. Cover the container with plastic wrap or slip the container into a plastic bag and close it. This covering is to reduce evaporation and provide miniature green house conditions of high humidity for rapid germination. As soon as the seeds germinate, you must remove the cover because the young seedlings require air and light.

FERTILIZING

Fertilizing of the tiny seedlings is necessary because the sterile medium does not contain any plant food. Use a liquid fertilizer once a week. Use a weak solution and use it sparingly. Always do a bit of watering before applying the fertilizer.

TRANSPLANTING

If, despite your efforts to plant sparsely, the seedlings are too thick, thin them immediately, using your fingers or tweezers to pluck them out gently with root structure intact for setting out in another container. As soon as true leaves (as distinguished from seed leaves) develop, you can set the seedlings in individual peat pots for direct transplanting outdoors. Of course, this is not mandatory and you may transplant vigorous seedlings directly from the seedbed to their permanent location once you have hardened them off. (*Hardening off* is the process of adapting plants to withstand lower temperatures after being grown indoors. This is accomplished by less watering and gradual exposure to outdoor conditions.)

Seedlings with first true leaves ready for transplanting.

To transplant seedlings, loosen them carefully with a small paring knife blade. Pick individual plants gently from the container, make a slit with the knife blade in the soil in the new container, insert the plant in the slit and firm the soil around it very carefully. Then water the newly transplanted seedlings by placing the container in a tub of tepid water until moisture glistens on the surface of the soil. The watering ensures that no pockets of air remain around the roots. Good contact of roots with soil is essential for vigorous growth. Continue to use a weak solution of liquid fertilizer sparingly on the transplanted seedlings.

TEMPERATURE

While waiting for the seeds to germinate, a temperature of sixty-five to seventy-five degrees is desirable—in other words, normal house temperatures. After germination, move the containers into a basement, garage, or cool bedroom where temperatures range between fifty and sixty degrees in order to have plants that are vigorous and stocky. Higher temperatures are conducive to fast growth, resulting in spindly, fragile plants. Remember that sunlight or artificial light is a necessary ingredient for vigorous plant growth. Seedlings grown on a window sill tend to lean toward the source of light; frequent turning of the container will offset this tendency.

"HARDENING-OFF"

As the plants increase in size and the time approaches for setting them outdoors in the garden, it become necessary to harden them off. This is done to lessen the shock of abruptly moving the plant from an indoor to an outdoor environment. Start this process by exposing the plants to outdoor conditions for two hours; avoiding direct rays of hot sun and windy spots. Double outdoor exposure time each day and at the same time reduce the amount of watering. Watering is best done in the morning so that plants are not soaking wet at night when the temperature drops. After a week of hardening-off, your plants are ready to be transplanted to the garden.

Started Plants

Tomatoes, pepper, cabbage, eggplant, broccoli, and many other vegetables are usually grown from plants that have been started from seed and grown by nursery-men for four to ten weeks before being set out in one's garden. For the small garden plot, it is far easier to purchase these plants locally than to start them from seed. Plants offered locally are adapted to your area and are usually of best quality. A family of four will be adequately supplied with fresh tomatoes and peppers that are produced from about eight to twelve well-tended plants of each type. In the space of one short growing season you will be able to decide what you want to grow and the approximate quantity of each item that you would like to harvest.

Transplanting

The term "transplanting" means moving plants from one location to another and does not really differ from the operation of planting. Transplanting usually results in a temporary slowdown of growth. The shock to the plant of changing locations can be mitigated by several means; one is to add a starter solution to the water you use to settle the soil around the roots of the plant. The water eliminates any air pockets that may exist and assures good contact of roots with the soil.

An excellent starter solution can be made by mixing two ounces of a commercial fertilizer in a gallon of water. Use 5-10-5, 5-10-10, or 10-10-10. Stir the mixture vigorously several times to get all the nutrients dissolved in the water. When setting out plants, first use plain water to settle the soil around the roots; then pour a cupful of the starter solution into the hole around the plant. Finish filling in the soil and pour in additional water to assist in settling the soil around the plant. If the soil is moist, you may omit this final bit of watering after using the starter solution. This solution is a good liquid fertilizer readily available for plant nourishment.

Set out plants in the evening so they do not have to withstand the full force of a hot sun on their first day in the new spot. Shading by means of anything that will cast a shadow is beneficial to plants just set out, especially if the soil is very dry, the sun is very hot, or the plants are beginning to wilt badly. Naturally, the most critical time for a plant is the first week it is exposed to the elements in a new location. If the plants do not appear to be vigorous and are not thriving in their new environment, water them generously after sundown. Protection from the direct rays of a hot sun for a day or two, coupled with generous watering after sundown will keep your plants alive and thriving.

It is well to remember that plants *are* alive. While waiting to set them out, protect them from the sun and the wind, and keep them moist, unless you store them in your refrigerator. Even while setting them out, protect them from the direct rays of the sun and the drying effect of wind by covering each plant (loosely) with a wet burlap bag or similar material.

Plants can be kept in a refrigerator at temperatures of $32°$ F. to $45°$ F. for short periods. Never store them in a freezer. Plants received in a wilted condition may be revitalized by putting them in a bucket and covering the roots with cold water for a few hours. "Puddling" the plants or "heeling" them in are very effective ways to hold them for future planting. *Puddling* is the process of working soil with water to make a mixture to coat roots of plants in order to keep them in good condition, temporarily, while holding them for future planting. *Heeling in* is a way of holding plants in the soil while waiting to set them in permanent locations.

Watering

Plants require about an inch of rainfall a week for best growth in most areas. If the rainfall is inadequate and moisture in the soil is depleted, you must provide water to ensure good production. A good soaking once a week is far better than daily sprinkling. In fact, light sprinkling is actually harmful inasmuch as it causes roots to seek the surface for the bit of water supplied. The best way to water your garden is to run the water in furrows between rows until the ground is well-soaked. For small plots use a sprinkler or a bucket and a cup. Watering your plants in a haphazard fashion and inadequately may do more harm than good. Late evening is the best time for watering inasmuch as the sun will not evaporate the water before it sinks into the soil.

You can easily make provisions for deep irrigation around a few tomato, pepper, or eggplants by cutting the tops and bottoms out of some tin cans, digging holes adjacent to the plants, and putting the cans in the holes. Make the tops level with the surface and then fill with gravel or small stones. Water poured into the can will provide moisture down at the roots where it is most effective. Keep filling the can until the water is no longer being quickly absorbed by the soil. This method of watering plants will encourage deep root structure, thereby enabling plants to better withstand heat and drought. Naturally, this method of watering is not limited to a few individual plants and may be employed as extensively as desired. The moral here is: do not permit lack of rain to ruin your garden. You may also feed your plants with liquid fertilizer by this method of watering.

Cultivation

Some people cannot bear the thought of pulling up healthy plants and casting them aside. Consequently, their plants are always too crowded and never bear heavy crops nor yield top-quality vegetables. Adequate spacing between plants is necessary for the leaves to draw nutrients from the air and receive the beneficial rays of the sun as well as to give the roots adequate room to draw nutrients from the soil. For a plant to enjoy its best environment, no other plant or weed must be allowed to encroach on its ground or air space. Thus, cultivation and weeding insures that the plant can take full advantage of the nutrients around it. When a plant can take full advantage of the fertility of the soil and does not have to share the nutrients with weeds, a healthier, more productive plant results.

The practice of cultivating one's plants as soon after a rain as the ground can be worked is the best means of controlling weeds. This kills sprouted weeds and loosens the soil so that it readily absorbs the next rainfall. Care should be exercised in hoeing in order not to injure plants. Hand weeding is very effective on small plots, and can be used close to plants on any size plot. It is best done after a rain when the soil is soft and weeds can easily be pulled out by the roots.

Insecticides

Most insects that damage vegetable plants may be effectively controlled with chemicals known as *insecticides.* There is a bewildering variety of insecticides on the market. However, one need not become a chemist nor study the habits of the various insect pests that chew the leaves, suck the sap, and occasionally cut off the stalk of a plant. Fortunately for the gardener, an all-purpose insecticide can be used on all the vegetables grown in the average garden, and it will be effective on approximately 99 percent of the garden pests encountered. Such an all purpose insecticide is Carbaryl (it is sold under several brand names). It is a 50 percent WP (wettable powder). Carbaryl is a synthetic carbomate that acts as a stomach poison as well as a contact insecticide.

Two tablespoonsful per gallon of water is the recommended spray mixture for everything in your garden. This means that you do not have to change from a weaker to a stronger mixture, or vice versa, when you finish spraying the bush beans for Mexican bean beetles and then decide you should spray the summer squash because you have just noticed some squash bugs. This insecticide can be a real labor- and time-saving convenience.

The many uses of Carbaryl have to be seen to be appreciated; here is a partial listing:

1. *Beans*—for control of Mexican bean beetle, leafhopper, lygus and stink bugs. May be applied up to one day before harvest.
2. *Corn*—for control of corn earworm, sap beetle, and Japanese beetle. May be applied up to one day before harvest on sweet corn ears for human consumption.
3. *Cucumbers and Summer Squash*—for control of striped and

spotted cucumber beetles, squash bugs, flea beetles, pickle-worm, and melonworm. May be applied up to day of harvest.

4. *Tomato, Eggplant, and Pepper*—for control of tomato fruit-worm, fall armyworm, and flea beetle. May be applied up to one day before harvest.

5. *Strawberries*—for control of meadow spittlebug and strawberry leaf roller. May be applied up to one day before harvest.

Carbaryl is equally effective on lettuce, cabbage, and most all fruits.

For small gardens, insecticides can be applied with a minimum amount of equipment, either by dusting or spraying. Some of the dusts can be applied by shaking the powder onto the plants, although this is effective only for small areas. You can also use a plunger-type duster with capacities from one to three pounds. They are usually constructed so you can easily spray the undersides of leaves. Carbaryl and Malathion with 4 percent of active ingredients are good all-purpose dusts for the vegetable garden. Apply an even, light coating of dust, in still air, and force it through the foliage in order to reach both sides of the leaves.

Dusting can only be done when there is relatively low wind.. Dust is more easily washed off by rain; it is also more expensive to dust than it is to spray. The most effective method of applying insecti-cides for the average gardener is by use of the small plunger-type sprayer. However, spraying cannot be done effectively when the foliage of the plant is wet with dew, whereas this is an ideal time for dusting. For the person with a small outdoor garden or with plants growing in containers, there are hand atomizers that come in many sizes, from approximately a pint to three quarts.

The small-scale gardener should not become too concerned with insecticides and spraying. The large-scale gardener, however, who is interested in spraying, should look into the advantages of a three- or four-gallon sling-type hand sprayer.

Fill your new sprayer (or old sprayer at the beginning of the season) with clean water and try it out before using an insecticide in it. Occasionally oil the pump plunger leather.

Empty your sprayer as soon as the job is finished and rinse it out thoroughly with clean water. You can prolong the life of your equipment by spraying some clean water through the hose and nozzle after you clean the tank. This, of course, rids the small channels and orifices of any particles of spray mixture that may have settled out. Hang the sprayer upside down, with pump removed, so it can drain and thoroughly dry out. Replace the pump in the tank as soon as the tank is dry. Mud daubers and other insects will inhabit the tank if it is left open. Rust inside the tank and tiny foreign objects in the spray mixture are your only hazards.

For your insect spray to be effective it is necessary to mix it in exactly the recommended proportions, keeping the solution agitated to prevent settling while it is being used. Spray the undersides of leaves where insects deposit their eggs and do most of their sucking and chewing damage.

The primary idea to to apply the spray where the trouble is; and to spray only to the point of run-off, using a fine cone-shaped mist. Drenching with its attendant run-off is wasteful and not as good for your plants as a fine covering of mist-like droplets.

Remember these points when spraying and dusting: in spraying, try to coat the foliage with a fine mist, without drenching, which results in "run-off;" when dusting, try to cover the foliage with a light cloud of the dust, as it is more effective and less damaging than a heavy application of powder.

If you are vigilant and spot insects when they first appear and start feasting on your plants, the battle is already half won. Wipe out these first few and you will have fewer insects to contend with all summer long.

Remember that improper use of insecticides can be injurious to plants, man, and animals. Heed all precautions and follow directions very carefully. The labels list both the vegetables the products are to be used on and the varieties of insects they will control. If you are purchasing the product for the first time, read the labels of the various brands. If you are still in doubt, get the opinion of your seedsman or nurseryman. Avoid inhalation of the insecticide and wash immediately after handling.

Beneficial Insects

Certain insects do not damage garden plants; instead, they destroy other insects that are injurious to vegetables. One of the best known is the praying mantis, which devours beetles, aphids, cutworms and other insects. Praying mantis egg cases (approximately 300 eggs) may be purchased from some mail order seed outlets for a very nominal amount. Ladybugs also devour larvae and worms of many harmful insects. A half-pint of ladybugs, about 5,000, can be purchased for less than five dollars. These insects can be used for natural control of garden pests. Among the many other beneficial insects are included lady beetles, ground beetles, spiders and mites, and the ant lion (doodlebug).

The mere presence of these beneficial insects is reason enough to deter one from preventative or indiscriminate spraying or dusting. In fact, when close observation of plants reveals very few pests, simply pick them off by hand and check again on succeeding days to determine if spraying or dusting is necessary.

Fungicides

Fungicides are used to control or prevent plant diseases such as early blight, leaf spot, seed decay, damping-off, late blight, and black rot. However, fungicides will not eradicate all plant diseases and one of the best measures is to pull up and burn all diseased plants. Treatment of seeds with Captan (Captan 50-W), Thiram (Arasan 75, Thiram-50), or Dichlone (Phygon Seed Protectant) is effective in preventing seed decay and damping-off. This treatment is a standard procedure for certified seed.

The best known fungicides are Copper and Organic. Do not let the many varieties lead you astray. Read the labels and if you're still undecided get the advice of the closest nurseryman or your country agricultural agent.

Just as is the case with insecticides, you do not need to study plant pathology to become a successful gardener. Many of our ancestors living in rural surroundings often produced more than 95 percent of their annual supply of food. Yet they were totally unacquainted with insecticides and fungicides as we know them today. Furthermore, their seeds were quite inferior to those available today both in percentage of germination and resistance to disease. And most hybrids in the vegetable world did not exist at that time. So, why not garden for the sheer joy of it and not become burdened with the negative side of the project? A positive "can-do" attitude, coupled with close observation of what is happening to your plants, can be your biggest asset in your gardening endeavor. It is worth remembering that seeds do not know if they are being handled by an amateur or an old pro; consequently, many beginners have splendid results simply because they follow directions carefully and observe their plants closely.

Legume Inoculation

Some plants of the pea family will not grow satisfactorily unless large numbers of certain nitrogen-fixing bacteria are present in the soil. Bacteria are obtained from a healthy legume root nodule and cultures are grown in a laboratory. These bacteria are prepared for particular legumes and the seeds are inoculated just before planting. The bacteria make atmospheric nitrogen available to the plant. The plant, in turn, supplies food to the bacteria on its roots and this causes rapid multiplication of the bacteria. This interaction is known as *symbiosis.*

Some of the legumes are very dependent on these nitrogen-fixing bacteria and simply will not produce a good crop where these bacteria are not present in large numbers in the soil. Alfalfa is a typical example of a leguminous crop requiring large numbers of the proper strain of bacteria for the very best yields. Consequently, seed inoculation is most desirable.

Inoculation of seed is particularly important when planting a crop of something new in a field for the first time—soybeans, for example. If soybeans have never been grown in that soil, the nitrogen-fixing bacteria will not be present in large enough numbers to ensure best plant growth and maximum production of beans. Yields have been increased 10 to 25 percent by seed inoculation with proper strains of bacteria.

Legume bacteria are easily applied to seeds moistened with water. Plant seeds immediately after treating to reduce chances of bacterial loss due to exposure to air and heat.

Harvesting

The natural act of harvesting is the payoff for our gardening effort.

The shortest time from garden to table produces the best flavor and nutritional content. This time element is also a vital factor for top quality in canning and freezing; the quicker it is done the better quality you will have. Vegetables deteriorate rapidly after being harvested, as evidenced by some of the wilted, tasteless produce encountered at the supermarkets.

Disturb the plants as little as possible when harvesting vegetables. For example, bush and pole beans should not be harvested when the leaves are wet. Cucumber and squash vines are easily damaged and one should restrain the vine or plant when plucking the fruit. Eggplant is so securely attached that it must always be cut from the bush.

The bearing season of almost all vegetables can be prolonged by harvesting them just as soon as they attain maximum growth for flavor and tenderness. This is especially applicable to squash, peppers, eggplant, tomatoes, cucumbers, okra, bush snap beans, and pole beans. If the seeds within these vegetables are allowed to ripen and mature, the plants and vines will either quit bearing entirely or there will be a drastic slowdown in production. Consequently, in order to keep your garden at peak production, you *must* harvest these vegetables at the proper time. Failure to do this will result in crops of inferior quality followed by a drastic reduction in quantity.

The green or snap bean provides a classic example of when to harvest. The mature pod varies from four to nine inches in length, depending on the variety. Some pods are round and some are flat; most are green, although some are yellow, and there is even a purple variety. Descriptions on individual seed packets and in seed catalogs provide information about size and color; these are good harvesting clues.

Many people insist on picking green beans when the young beans are just starting to form in the pod, and when the pod is less than two-thirds of its full-grown length. Granted, they are delicious at this stage; however, if you were to harvest all your green beans at this stage of growth you would be wasting about one-half of your crop due to reduced size and weight. Years of close observation and critical sampling of the chef's best efforts have convinced this writer that the quality and flavor of the full-grown bean is not inferior to that of the immature pod. In fact, some varieties do not acquire their best flavor until they are full-grown. So start picking the young pods when you can no longer resist the temptation, and always pick those pods that are closest to full-grown. If the pods are left on the bushes after they reach full maturity, the pods will change color, shrivel a bit, and harden. If some of your green beans reach this stage shell them and spread them out to dry in any well-ventilated area. When they are dry, store them in suitable containers for future use as dry beans.

One can easily and readily determine when green beans are in prime condition by the bright color of the pods and by the ease with which they snap apart when quickly bent in the middle. Beware of dull-colored, full-podded, rubbery beans that fail to snap apart when bent double.

You have several options with a surplus of vegetables—these include canning, freezing, and temporary storage in the refrigerator (bearing in mind that most vegetables purchased at the supermarket have been harvested from one to two weeks before you even see them). Of course, you can always share the surplus with some friend or neighbor.

Canning and Preserving

The recent "back to nature" trend came at a time when the ancient arts of preserving and storing vegetables seemed destined to be lost amongst supermarket shelves crammed with convenience foods. People are beginning to realize that the ability to be self-sufficient brings not only satisfaction, but a sense of security. Furthermore, you cannot "buy" the flavor and nutrition that you can get from freezing or canning your own vegetables.

The methods used to preserve vegetables and fruits are the very epitome of simplicity and convenience. Here are a few examples for your consideration.

LEATHER BREECHES BEANS

Use only select, tender green beans. Take a three- or four-foot length of strong thread and tie a kitchen match stem (or similar--sized piece of wood) onto one end and put the other end through a long needle. Push the needle through the center of the bean, pushing the beans together down against the other end of the thread, filling from end to end. The beans will dry better if they alternate in layers at right angles to each other. Hang the string on a nail or rafter in a warm, airy space, but never in direct sunlight. The direct rays of the sun rob them of some of their flavor. Keep them hanging until the beans are thoroughly dry. They are now dehydrated and will keep almost indefinitely if stored in a dry area. Store them in a paper bag or box until you are ready to use them.

When you get ready for a meal of leather breeches, remove the string and drop your dried green beans into a pot of boiling water. Add one or two pieces of salt pork and cook for two or three hours. Add just enough hot water to keep them covered while cooking and take care not to cook them too long. An occasional sampling will let you know when they are at their best—tender, but not mushy, not overcooked.

APPLES

Apples may be thinly sliced and strung on thread exactly the same as green beans. Or the apples may be cored, then sliced and put on thin poles. The apples to be dried are hung in the sun or around a source of heat. If they are outdoors, they should be brought inside at sundown. The drying process takes from three to five days, depending on the temperature and relative humidity. The sliced apples become brown and rubbery while becoming dehydrated. When dry, they may be stored in sacks or boxes, in a dry area, for winter use.

Use the dried apples for frying, desserts, and pies. You may be pleasantly surprised to find they have retained all of their delicious flavor.

PICKLED BEANS

String beans are broken, any strings removed, washed and then cooked for a few minutes until barely tender. Soak in cold water until thoroughly chilled and pack them tightly in a clean crock jar. Add enough salty water to cover the beans. Use one-half cup of salt (do not use iodized salt for pickling) per gallon of water. Cover the beans with a dinner plate or a piece of heavy aluminum foil and they will be ready for table use in about two weeks. They may be used directly from the crock and will remain good for several months. Exclude light from top of crock and store in a cool place.

4
Basic
Vegetables
for
Your Garden

Beans

The average gardener thinks of only two types of beens—green beans and limas. The green bean often called *snap* is stringless or nearly so in the best varieties. The snap bean grows in two main types, bush (low) or pole. Both types are highly productive, but the pole bean will produce more in a given ground space and the beans are more easily harvested. The pole variety will climb a trellis or fence or a hill of corn and does not necessarily require a pole if planted near these supports. If a pole is used for support, it must be firmly planted in the ground. A small sapling seven or eight feet long and about two inches in diameter will be satisfactory. Leave the bark on it and do not trim too smoothly, as any projections aid the beans in climbing.

Green beans are well grown on land that has received a generous application of fertilizer or manure. However, a top dressing of fertilizer when the plants are about a foot high is conducive to heavy yields if the plants have not been grown in excessively fertile soil. (See page 16 for a discussion of top dressing.) When the plants have reached a foot in height, it is of inestimable value to bank soil around the plants to a depth of three or four inches. Use your bare hands or a hoe, but be careful not to injure the roots. The banking of soil around the plants assists in moisture retention, retards weeds, and is good cultivation.

Beans should not be planted until the ground is warm. This is usually about two weeks after the last killing frost in your area. However, successive plantings may then be made at two or three week intervals until about two months before the first frost in the fall.

If hand cultivation is used, make the rows eighteen inches apart. Trace the furrows two inches deep and space the beans two to three inches apart in the row. Cover with fine soil about one inch deep in heavy soil and about one and one-half inches deep in light soil. Firm the soil gently to assist in germination. On every heavy soil it is a good idea to cover the beans in the furrow with a mixture of sand, light humus, and peat or other suitable material that will not bake or form a hard crust.

When the seeds have germinated and the plants are two to four inches high, thin them to stand with about four inches between plants. However, it is best not to handle or cultivate bean plants when they are wet; all evidence indicates that this is likely to spread disease.

POLE BEANS

Pole beans are planted and cultivated in a manner similar to the low or bush type. Plant five or six beans in a circle around the pole and when they are well-started thin to two or three plants per pole. Poles should be three to four feet apart each way. Pole beans alongside a trellis or fence should be six inches apart. When corn stocks are used for support, wait until the corn is about three inches high then plant the beans around the hill of corn. It is well to help the bean tendrils get started around and up the support, remembering that they tend to twine in a counterclockwise direction.

Fordhook 242 bush lima beans are vigorous, productive, and heat-resistant.

LIMA BEANS

Limas need a longer growing season than snap beans and cannot safely be planted until after the ground is thoroughly warm, usually about two weeks after snap beans are planted. Both the large and small-seeded lima beans are available in bush and pole varieties. Planting and cultivation are the same as for string or snap beans— bearing in mind that higher temperatures and longer growing seasons are required.

GREEN-SHELL BEANS

The Long Pod Fava (English Broad Bean) is a hardy bush bean that can be used as a substitute for pole limas in the northern parts of the country with short growing seasons. Fava beans are much hardier than other beans and may be planted early, at the same time as peas, as soon in the spring as the ground can be worked. The plants are true bush form, heavy yielders, large, and erect. Pods are glossy green, about seven inches long, and contain from five to seven large, oblong-shaped, flat, light green beans with a flavor a bit like that of the pea. The beans resemble limas and should be used in the same way.

Even if you are not planting the Fava as a substitute for the pole lima, you should still consider this bean because you can be eating it in the middle of June—long before your other beans mature. (Date of first harvesting is naturally dependent on local climatic conditions and date of planting.)

Tendercrop is a mosaic-resistant, heavy yielding snap bean with tender, round, green pods and a wide range of adaptability.

Sow in rows, placing the seed about five inches apart in the row and covering with three inches of soil. Rows should be one and one-half to two and one-half feet apart, depending on the space available and the method of cultivation. When they are up and growing, thin to stand ten to twelve inches apart.

Dwarf horticultural is another green-shell bean with outstanding qualities; it is delicious, either green or dried.

There are literally hundreds of varieties of beans, and some are vastly superior. Outstanding varieties of bush beans include the following: Tenderpod, Tendercrop, Topcrop, Romano 14, and Lika Lake. Pole varieties that are adaptable to most conditions and give high yields are Kentucky Wonder, Romano (Italian Pole), Blue Lake, and McCaslan.

You will never really appreciate the bountiful yield and exquisite flavor of freshly harvested green beans until you pick them from your own bean patch.

Peas

Peas are a cool-weather crop and should be planted as early in the spring as the ground can be worked. For a longer yield, make successive plantings at ten-day intervals or plant an early and a main crop variety at the same time. The average gardener will probably prefer the low or dwarf varieties that grow fifteen to twenty-four inches high and require no support. However, it must be noted that peas grown on supports are less liable to destruction by birds and frequently produce higher yields.Peas are usually planted in double rows about three inches apart with seeds spaced about two inches apart and covered with one to two inches of fine soil. Space the double rows about two and one-half feet apart. The only cultivation required is to pull any weeds that appear. For the taller varieties of peas that grow to a height of as much as six feet one must provide some kind of support. Tree branches may be stuck into the ground at sufficient intervals to provide a climbing area. If branches are not available, one may plant a pole at the end of each row between the furrows and run heavy twine or cord from pole to pole, beginning about a foot from the ground and on to the top at one-foot intervals. It is to be noted that dwarf varieties may give only one picking—in general, the taller the vine, the longer the picking season.

EDIBLE-PODDED PEAS
(SUGAR PEAS)

Sugar peas have the tenderness and fleshy-podded qualities of a snap bean combined with the flavor and sweetness of fresh green peas. When they are young, cook them like snap beans, pods and all. At this stage, the pods are free of fiber, succulent, brittle, and stringless. If the pods develop too fast for use as snap beans, seeds may be used as shell peas and are at their flavor peak before reaching full size. Planting is the same as for other varieties of peas. Dwarf Gray Sugar is one of the earliest, dwarfest, and best.

COWPEAS

Also known as black-eye peas or Southern table peas, cowpeas are easily grown, tasty, and highly nutritious. Plant after all danger of frost is past and ground is warm because they are susceptible to cold. Sow the seed in furrows two inches deep and space the seed two to three inches apart in the row. Space the rows three feet apart. When plants are about three inches high, thin to stand four to six inches apart. Keep surface soil cultivated and weed free but avoid handling and cultivations of plants when they are moist with dew or rain.

Considering the effort necessary to grow them, few if any other vegetables will yield higher dividends. Well-known varieties are Monarch and California Blackeye, White Acre, Brown Crowder, and DixiLee.

Beets

Beets are both tolerant of heat and cold and may be planted as much as four weeks before the last frost-free date. They are rich feeders and good quality depends on quick growth. Quick growth results from friable land with plenty of plant nutrients. Top dressing when plants are about six inches high tends to speed growth. What appears to be a beet seed is actually a little crinkled ball containing several seeds. Inasmuch as beet plants should be spaced three inches apart in the row, one of those crinkly balls every three inches will ensure germination and thinning will be reduced to a minimum. Make furrows one inch deep and cover with no more than one inch of fine soil. Rows can be fifteen to eighteen inches apart. Do whatever thinning is required when the plants are two to three inches tall and well established. Beets may be sown at three-week intervals to ensure a fresh, prime supply for the table. It is best to sow fifteen-foot rows and not have beets maturing sooner than they can be used to good advantage.

Carrots

Carrot seeds are very small and germination is quite slow. The mature plants need very little space between them. Consequently, one may grow five or six per foot of row. Place the seeds in shallow furrows about two per inch and cover with half an inch of fine, screened soil. Thin to two inches apart when they are two inches tall. Care in sowing the seed greatly lessens the labor of thinning.

Parsnips

Parsnips do best in deep, fertile, loamy soil. Seed should be sown as early in the spring as the ground can be worked. The seeds are slow to germinate and the percentage of germination is low; accordingly, sow them thickly and thin as required to stand about four inches apart. Radishes sown thinly in the row will mark the row, thus allowing for one or two cultivations between rows before the parsnips are up. Sow the seeds thickly in a shallow furrow, covering with fine soil to a depth of one-half inch. Rows may be fifteen to thirty inches apart, depending on the method of cultivation.* Germination is assisted by covering the seed with something that will not harden and bake, such as a mixture of leaf mold and sand or peat and topsoil. Firming the soil after applying will also improve contact and help germination.

Parsnips have a distinctive flavor that is always improved by cold weather. They may be left in the ground and harvested as needed. However, they should be mulched to prevent alternate freezing and thawing. They are among the most nutritious and most flavorful of the root crops. Hollow Crown and All-American are the best-known varieties.

---

*Fifteen to eighteen inches apart for hand cultivation and thirty inches apart for machine cultivation.

Squash

Squash are best divided into two main types—summer squash and winter squash.

SUMMER SQUASH

We are primarily concerned with summer squash for their fresh use at the table. The summer types include the Summer Crookneck, the Straightneck, the Bush Scallop (Cymling), and the vegetable marrows. All of these squashes must be used while young and tender. A good test is that the rind must be soft enough to easily pierce with the thumbnail. All summer varieties should be gathered before the rinds harden and the seeds ripen.

A mulched plant of Yellow Straightneck summer squash.

Well-rotted cow manure thoroughly mixed with the soil or commercial fertilizer is recommended. A good plan is to remove about a bucketful of soil and thoroughly mix it with a like amount of well-rotted cow manure. If you are using commercial fertilizer, remove a bucketful or two of soil and thoroughly mix about a pound (a pint) of fertilizer with half the removed soil. Replace the fertilized mixture and firm it well to provide good capillary action. Then cover the mixture with about four inches of soil.

Space the hills about four feet apart each way for the bush varieties. Unless you have unlimited space, stay away from the running vine type of squash. When the ground starts to warm and all danger of frost is past, put four or five seeds in each hill and cover with one inch of fine soil. When plants are up and growing, thin to two or three of the most vigorous.

The bush-type hybrid zucchinis are highly recommended. Four hills will provide an adequate supply for a family of four.

WINTER SQUASH

Winter squash take much longer to attain maturity and must remain on the vine until fully matured. They must be harvested before hard frosts, leaving an inch or so of the stem attached to the fruit. Winter squash are easily stored in a dry, moderately warm area. They are hard-shelled fruits and are used extensively for canning, boiling, baking, and "pumpkin" pie. Planting and cultivation is similar to the summer squash.

Popular varieties include True Hubbard, Gold Nugget, Golden Delicious, Waltham Butternut, Boston Marrow, and Table Queen or Acorn. Average time to reach maturity is 80 to 115 days depending on the variety planted. It is essential that you consider the first expected frost date and plant your winter squash in time to reach maturity prior to this date.

Cucumber

Cucumbers are a warm-weather crop requiring lots of moisture, plenty of heat, and a rich soil. Remove two buckets of soil from an area fifteen to eighteen inches in diameter and replace one bucket of soil with a bucketful of well-rotted cow or horse manure. Firm the manure and cover with remaining soil, firming it to ensure good capillary action. Seed should be four inches or more from the manure. If you are using commercial fertilizer, thoroughly mix a pound with a bucketful of soil; replace this mixture, firming it well. Replace the remaining soil, being sure to have three or four inches of soil between the seed and the fertilizer. Plant six seeds in each group, planning on thinning to half that number when plants are growing vigorously. Cover the seed to a depth of about one-half inch. The cucumber plant is a sprawling, tendril-bearing vine that likes to roam in all directions. Consequently, gardeners with small plots are frequently advised not to try to grow them. However, most of them are climbers and may be grown on a trellis or a fence. A teepee or tripod arrangement of three to six poles tied together at the top and secured over the hills or groups will keep the vines from sprawling and covering too large an area. Fasten the vines to the poles loosely by means of inch or so widths of soft cloth. Old nylons and old sheets make excellent cucumber ties. Remember that the vines are tender; be careful lest you injure them while handling.

Cucumbers may be harvested at any size, depending on their intended use. Both standard and hybrid varieties are vigorous and productive. If you standard variety does not grow vigorously, or if it appears to be bothered with disease, you should consider a hybrid that is resistant to mildew and mosaic.

Downy mildew is spread by windblown spores and is rather easy to control with either Maneb or Zineb. It is usually identified by the appearance of black spots on the leaves, frequently accompanied by a gray fungus on the opposite side of the leaf and directly beneath the black spot.

Mosaic is a virus disease that causes a yellowing on either side of the veins of a leaf. This chlorosis is a failure to produce the normal green coloring matter in leaves, causing them to become yellowish, pale, and resulting in an unhealthy plant. It may be spread from diseased plants to healthy plants by insects (aphids) or by rubbing against the plants with tools.

Good standard varieties of cucumber are Straight Eight, White Spine, and Sunnybrook. Excellent hybrids are M&M, Burpeeana, Surecrop, and the Burpless. Primarily for pickling are small-size varieties such as National Pickling, Wisconsin SMR 18, Ohio MR 17, and Burpee Pickler.

Onions

Onions do best in a well-drained, rich soil. They thrive under varied conditions of climate and soil due to their tolerance of cold and heat and their vigor. The soil should be fine and free of stones, clods, and foreign matter. Both well-rotted manure and fertilizer should be used. About a pound of manure to each square foot of ground and about five pounds of fertilizer to each one hundred square feet are about right.

Onions are easiest grown by using "sets." The set is a small, dried bulblet raised from seed the previous year and picked when young. Each bulblet will produce a mature onion during the season. Sets are used for the bunching type of spring onion that is eaten fresh. The sets are inexpensive in the amounts needed by the average gardener.

Sets should be planted in a two-inch furrow about two inches deep. When you start eating them, thin them to stand about four inches apart for those you want to grow to maturity. Keep the rows about fifteen inches apart—although, in small plots (well-fertilized) they may be grown successfully in rows as close as six inches.

It is necessary to cultivate them enough to keep down weeds and conserve soil moisture; however, the onion is a shallow-rooted crop and one must be careful not to injure the bulbs.

Chicken manure between the rows, gently worked into the soil, provides a valuable fertilizer for the onions due to its high nitrogen content.

The tops should be cut from harvested mature onions about an inch above the bulb. The onions should then be spread out in an airy space or on racks to dry off the surface moisture. This usually takes from one to two weeks. A good indicator of curing is when the cut-off stem is no longer green but shriveled. At this stage the onions may be safely stored in net sacks or airy crates in a well-ventilated, dry, cool room.

Chives

Chives are onion-scented perennial herbs that are widely adaptable and easily grown. They do not produce the typical bulbs of the onion and are grown for the hollow, cylindrical leaves, which are cut and used in salads, sauces, soups, and stews. Their mild onion flavor is sought by many. The leaves may be cut fine and sprinkled on meat and vegetables.

Chives are frequently planted as a border in flower beds or alongside walkways. They may be started from clumps of bulbs or seed. Once started, they are easy to propagate in new areas by moving some of the bulbs. They thrive in a window box or pot and provide an excellent source of seasoning all year long.

A pot of chives grown in a kitchen window.

Lettuce

Lettuce can be grown in any home garden, but superior quality can be produced in rich, moist, sandy loans. Adequate soil moisture will ensure quick growth if the soil is rich in plant food. To make the soil rich, mix about three wheelbarrow loads of well-rotted manure to fifty feet of row. In addition, use about three pounds of a commercial fertilizer. If only one of these is available, try to use the manure, simply because it adds humus to the soil, thus increasing its moisture-holding capacity in addition to enriching it. Lettuce is best grown in cool weather; throughout much of the country lettuce culture is limited to spring and autumn.

There are many varieties of lettuce that do well under the right conditions of soil and moisture. Of the loose leaf kinds, Black-Seeded Simpson, Green Ice, Saladbowl, Slobolt, and Grand Rapids are among the best. Slobolt and Saladbowl are heat-resistant and desirable for culture in warm weather.

Saladbowl lettuce is an outstanding leaf lettuce with considerable heat resistance.

Lettuce can be sown in the spring as early as the ground can be worked, or even when the ground is only a little dry on the surface. Sow the seed thinly in shallow furrows about one and one-half feet apart and cover with one-half inch of fine soil. As plants show vigor and growth, gradually thin to one-half to one foot apart to give plants room to spread and to prolong the cutting season.

Mustard Greens

Mustard is cold-hardy and widely adaptable. It is related to the turnip and is cultivated in the same manner. The two bear a close resemblance. Mustard greens are a bit more pungent than turnip greens and contain about the same vitamin and mineral content.

Sow the seed early in the spring, rather thickly, and begin the thinning process when the plants are in full leaf and about six inches tall. Naturally, you will use these thinnings. A twenty-foot row followed by successive plantings at two-week intervals will soon indicate to you both the time between plantings and length of rows. Best flavor is before the leaves are full-grown and before much reddish-brown color appears around the edges of the leaves.

The mustard plant does not thrive in hot weather, so terminate your successive plantings before the heat of summer. Resume planting in August and make successive sowings for use in autumn and fall.

Mustard greens, under favorable conditions, mature in thirty-five to forty-five days and provide an excellent and easy source of nutritious "boiling greens." Common varieties include Tender-green, Southern Curled, Fordhook Fancy, and Florida Broadleaf.

Kale

Kale is cold-hardy and lives through winter as far north as the Pennsylvania border and in other northern areas where similar climatic conditions exist.

Kale, a hardy green, is mulched here with spoiled hay.

It is also quite resistant to heat and may be grown in the summer. Kale responds to heat by leaf dryness and toughness; it responds to cold weather by becoming tender and succulent. Therefore, its real merit is as a cool-weather green. Kale is ideal for successive planting to follow some early-season vegetable such as peas, potatoes, or beets.

In the late summer or early fall, the seed may be broadcast very thinly and then very lightly raked into the soil. The best production is had by thinning stands that are too thick. Spring sowings are best made in rows one and one-half to two feet apart and then thinned to about a foot apart.

Kale is harvested by taking the larger leaves while young and continuing to take the lower ones that are in good condition and leaving the upper ones to reach further maturity. You may, of course, cut the entire plant and enjoy the tenderest leaves at the top near the rosette; but this is needless waste because the removal of a few prime leaves as required for the table does not harm the plant and it will continue to produce until its life cycle is ended.

Kale is widely used for "boiling greens" and the young leaves may be chopped raw like lettuce for use in salads and on sandwiches. It provides an excellent source of vitamin-rich greens that can be made available fresh from the garden on almost a year-round basis. With a little protection it will usually stand the average winter.

Well-known garden varieties are Blue Curled Scotch, Dwarf Siberian, and Vates Blue Curled.

Chard

Chard, or Swiss chard, is developed from the beet, but is used for its top instead of its root. It is cold-hardy and resistant to heat the same as kale. Like kale, it produces a continuous supply of leaves, which may be harvested as needed. The outer leaves may be harvested repeatedly without injury to the plant. Take the outer leaves from each plant and leave the inner ones to develop further. However, all the leaves may be cut off about four inches above the ground. Regardless of the method used to remove the leaves, the plant will respond with new growth. One row about forty feet long will supply a family of four the entire summer.

The culture of chard is identical to that of beets, except that the plants grow larger and should be thinned to six inches or more apart in the row.

Swiss chard is especially suitable for hot-weather culture.

Cabbage

Cabbage is one of the most important garden crops. It is widely adapted to different soils. It is a heavy feeder and requires plenty of moisture and good, fertile soil to produce quick growth and good quality. Well-rotted manure and commercial fertilizer should be liberally used. In addition to the fertilizing at planting, a top dressing of nitrate of soda or 34.5-0-0 is advisable once or twice during the growing season. For individual plants use about one-third of an ounce. The supplemental feeding with nitrates is not so important for late cabbage.

The beginning gardener would do best by obtaining his early plants from a nursery or seed supply. They may be set out as soon as the ground can be worked. Early varieties are usually set fourteen inches apart with the rows twice that far apart. Late season cabbage should be set two feet apart in the row, with rows three feet apart.

Late cabbage plants are grown in open seed beds. The seed should be planted about a month before the plants are needed. Late cabbage is prized for storage, kraut, and table use.

Early varieties are Golden Acre and Early Jersey Wakefield—both are yellows-resistant. Danish Ballhead, Premium Flat Dutch, and Wisconsin Hollander (yellows-resistant) are largely used for late planting.

Chinese cabbage is a desirable autumn crop in the Northern States.

Chinese Cabbage

The Chinese cabbage, or celery cabbage, is not related to celery and is more closely related to mustard than to cabbage. It may be served like lettuce or shredded into cole slaw. It is better than ordinary cabbage when boiled. The nonheading type is both delicious and nutritious. It is called Michihli, Crispy Choy, and Wong Bok.

Chinese cabbage appears to do best as an autumn crop and sowing of seed should be done about three months before first expected frost. This will provide "greens" until freezing weather prevails.

The cultivation and harvesting of Chinese cabbage is the same as that for chard. It is worth repeating that it is a cold-hardy plant and best results are to be had from seed sown two or three months before first expected frost. It tends to bolt if the seed is sown in the spring. *Bolting* is the term used to describe unwanted or premature production of flowers and seeds, often caused by deficiency in the soil or excessive heat. It occurs in Chinese cabbage, lettuce, and other plants.

New Zealand Spinach
(Hot Weather or Everlasting Spinach)

New Zealand spinach is much more tolerant of heat than ordinary spinach, and much easier to grow. Botanically, it is *Tetragonia expansa*—a native of New Zealand. It so greatly resembles spinach in appearance and flavor that most persons will not be aware of the difference. The strong plants produce an abundance of fleshy, brittle green leaves and young stem tips that can be picked repeatedly, as new leaves and stem tips are readily produced all during summer and fall, until the plants are killed by frost.

The seeds are large, very hard, and slow to germinate, taking from three to five weeks to come up (this is a good one to mark with radishes). Germination may be speeded up by soaking the seed in warm water for thirty-six hours to soften the hard shells. They may be sown as soon as danger of frost is past, one to two and one-half inches deep in the furrow. Plant seeds about six inches apart and one to one and one-half inches deep, but thin to stand about one and one-half or two feet apart in the row. Rows should be three to four feet apart because these plants are large and need lots of room.

These plants are so sturdy and so productive that four to six of them will provide ample spinach for a family of four. They are highly recommended for a continuous supply of fresh, nutritious, flavorful spinach. The plants respond generously to a scant top dressing of 10-10-10 or 34.5-0-0. And a top dressing of chicken manure gives excellent results due to its nitrogen content.

Parsley

Parsley is cold-hardy and at the same time able to withstand heat to the extent that it will continue to thrive throughout the summer. It is the most popular and best-known plant for garnishing and seasoning. It is widely adaptable and will thrive on any friable, fertile soil. The seeds are exceedingly slow to germinate. Germination may be hastened by soaking the seeds in water for twenty-four hours to forty-eight hours. Sow the seeds in a very shallow furrow, covering them to a depth of one-fourth inch or less. Covering the seed with a board until the first seedlings appear is beneficial and so is daily, gentle watering, being careful to sprinkle lightly so you will not disturb the tiny seed. A six-foot row is ample for one or two families. As the sprigs are pinched or cut off at the base, new growth appears. At the onset of winter, entire plants can be potted, moved indoors, and will provide parsley all winter long. It also makes an attractive house-plant. It may be carried through the winter in most of the north with a little protection.

Tomatoes

Tomatoes may be grown under a wide variety of conditions and do not require much space for a large yield. Best results are obtained from soil that has been well-prepared with manure or commercial fertilizer, or both. However, one should be aware of the fact that too much nitrogen may result in excessive vine growth and a failure to set many fruits. If you do encounter a lot of excess leaves, simply pinch or cut them off.

Tomato plants for the home garden may be grown from seeds started in a window box or similar container and the individual plants then transplanted to peat pots or paper drinking cups with bottoms removed. The seeds germinate best at ordinary house temperature. Seed must be started six to eight weeks before you plan

*Tomato plants staked with a wire cylinder to hold them off the
ground so the fruit does not rot. The grass mulch around the plants
controls weeds and conserves moisture.*

on setting the plant out in your garden. You are looking for plants
that are resistant to fusarium wilt and verticillium. The hybrids are
both disease-resistant and heavy producers.

Distance between plants depends to some extent on the variety
but more on staking and pruning. If you let the plants sprawl they
should be about three feet apart in rows about four feet apart. If
staked and pruned they may be planted as close as one and one-half
feet in the row, with rows three feet apart. Staked and pruned
tomatoes are advantageous in small garden plots and make for
easier cultivation, with easier to find, cleaner fruits.

Set the plants in the garden when all danger of frost is past. If
frost or freezing weather is forecast after you have set out tomato
plants, protect them overnight with hotkaps, tin cans, or paper
boxes placed over the plants. This will prevent the plants being
retarded by frostbite.

The time from setting out plants to harvest of ripe fruits will depend on the variety of tomato, condition of soil, and climate; however, the average will be from sixty to seventy days.

Plants purchased locally are adapted to your locality and are desirable if you do not want to start from seed. When buying, select strong, sturdy plants. In setting a plant into the ground, use a trowel to make a generous-sized hole and set the plant deeply (about two-thirds of it in the ground), filling carefully so as to not injure the roots. When the hole is almost full, pour water around the plant to settle the soil and to eliminate air pockets. A cup of starter solution poured around the plant at this time is beneficial in giving the plant a boost in its new location. Now finish putting soil around the plant. It is usually advantageous to leave a small depression around each plant for water to collect in, unless, of course, the soil is already too wet.

Staked plants will continue to develop extra foliage; consequently, one must continue to pinch off enough leaves so the sun can reach the developing fruit. Just before the first frost you may harvest the remaining green fruits and either let them ripen on a sunny window sill or wrap them individually in newspaper and store them in a cardboard box. The wrapped tomatoes will ripen in two to four weeks, depending on their size when harvested and the temperature of the room where they are stored.

Tomatoes should not be grown in the same area year after year. This is conducive to wilt disease, which can kill the plants. To check for fusarium wilt, break open the stem. If there are brown streaks just under the surface of the stem, the disease is present. The only way to successfully combat fusarium wilt is to change planting areas and use varieties that are disease-resistant.

Plants adapted to your locality are sold locally. However, you can exercise good judgment in selecting strong, sturdy, hybrid plants. If you have any doubts about the best varieties for your area, either check with your county agricultural agent or the state agricultural experimental station.

Exceptional results have been produced by using a double handful of well-rotted cow manure in the hole where the plant is set. Make the hole about six inches deeper than required for regular planting. Put the manure in the bottom of the hole and tamp it down firmly. Cover the manure with three or four inches of soil and firm the soil to assist in good capillary action. Try to have about two to three inches of soil between the roots of the plant and the manure.

Now go ahead and set the plant just as you would if there were no manure beneath it. When the roots grow enough to reach the manure the tomato plant will "suddenly" start growing vigorously and it will continue to show exceptional vigor throughout its life cycle. Do not become worried about fusarium wilt, verticillium, and blossom-end rot. Chances are that your tomato plants will be sturdy, vigorous, and produce lots of fruits. However, it is best to know that such things do exist and can occur. This should encourage you to use due care in selecting good varieties of disease-resistant plants.

The large green tomato hookworm can be controlled by merely picking it from the plant as they usually occur in small numbers. Its presence is indicated by the disappearance of the edges of the leaves. It has a voracious appetite and will devour lots of leaves in a hurry. Its green coloring serves as excellent camouflage and you will have to look closely to find them. Cutworm damage may be prevented by encircling the plant stem with a collar of stiff paper or plastic extending about an inch both above and below the soil. If cutworm damage is observed, scratch a small circle around each plant and look for the worms. Ususally one can locate and destroy them quite easily.

Well-established wilt-resistant varieties are Manalucie, Fireball, Marglobe, Rutgers, Moreton Hybrid, Homestead, Enterpriser, and Sioux.

Peppers

Peppers are hot weather plants and should not be set out until all danger of frost is past and the soil has begun to warm up. Both the pepper plant and the seed require a higher temperature than the tomato, although the writer has frequently set both of them out on the same day and grown them side by side.

You may purchase pepper plants and set them out when you set out your tomato plants. If you are trying to "rush the season" so to speak, you'd better wait another two or three weeks before setting out pepper plants. Handle your pepper plants exactly the way you take care of your tomato plants.

It is essential for you to know what kind of peppers you wish to raise. The mild-flavored peppers are sweet and are used for salads, stuffing, and slicing. Good varieties are California Wonder, Ruby King, Burpee's Tasty Hybrid, Yolo Wonder, King of the North, Emerald Giant, and Penn Wonder.

California Wonder variety of pepper.

Hot peppers that are used for flavoring, sauces, and pickling are represented by such varieties as Red Chili, Hungarian Wax, Long Red Cayenne, and Anaheim M.

There is still a third category of garden peppers, the pimiento. These are chiefly produced in California and the warmer sections of the South.

Eggplant

The eggplant is essentially a tropical plant that requires heat for its development. It is also called mad-apple, Jew's-apple, and aubergine. The plants should not be set outdoors until after the soil has warmed up and both day and night temperaturs are high. The handling of eggplant in the garden is the same as for tomatoes and peppers, except it is far more sensitive to cold than either of them.

Plant the same as tomatoes but top dress sparsely with commercial fertilizer within a week after setting out. Another top dressing when the plants start to bloom is beneficial.

Eggplant thrives best in a fertile, rich, moist, sandy loam. It will not thrive in heavy soils. The plants are large and bushy when mature, so set them three to four feet apart each way. A few plants will yield a large number of fruits; four to six plants would be about right for a family of four. The fruits are so heavy and so well-attached that they should be cut, not torn, from the plant.

Young plants are also quite sensitive to dryness. If timely rains do not provide adequate moisture, you can save both your plants and your investment in them by a good soaking at intervals of five days or so during the period of extreme dryness.

The fruits are at their best when the skin has a high gloss, just before they reach maximum size.

Good varieties are Black Beauty, Jersey King, Early Beauty Hybrid, Burpee Hybrid, and Florida Highbush.

The eggplant is a popular vegetable that requires little space.

Turnips

The turnip is one of the most widely grown root crops in the country. It is grown both for the root and the young tops, which make excellent greens. In our land of plenty, where they can be grown so easily, too many people think of turnips as food for the poor. The greens are rich in vitamins and minerals and contain far more Vitamins A and C and calcium on a cooked-volume basis than green beans or fresh garden peas.

Turnips do well in all parts of the country, and when planted after another crop they require no additional fertilizer. They are cold-hardy and may be grown in the spring and fall. In the spring, sow the seed as soon as the ground can be worked. Grow them in a row, make a very shallow furrow, drop the seed very thinly in it, and cover with one-eighth to one-fourth inch of soil. When the plants are up and growing, thin to stand two or three inches apart. The thinner the original sowing of seed, the less work required in thinning.

The Foliage or Shogoin turnips may be used for greens within thirty days—a bit sooner when one uses the final thinning for greens. Those grown for the root crop will be ready for the table in forty-five to seventy days. Here again, the time can be shortened by harvesting smaller roots, which are delicious.

Turnip seed may be broadcast and lightly raked in with a garden rake. The young tops of all varieties make good greens. Purple-Top White Globe, Tokyo Cross, and Just Right are the most desirable varieties. They are at their best when grown in cold weather and a tinge of frost seems to greatly improve their flavor. The plants stoutly resist the inroads of winter and the roots remain firm and good until temperatures drop so low that the soil remains frozen. Before this occurs, harvest the roots and store them where it is cool and dry, preferably between thirty and fifty-five degrees, covered with newspaeprs to exclude light. Under these conditions they can be kept for months.

Rutabaga

The rutabaga is a northern cousin of the turnip and requires about ninety days to mature. Rutabagas are sometimes referred to as "Canadian turnips" or "big yellow turnips." Some people seem to prefer the rutabaga flavor to that of the turnip.

They are excellent for table use and, reaching maturity after most garden vegetables are gone, are valued for their firm flesh and good flavor. The most desirable varieties are Improved Purple-Top and Purple-Top Yellow.

Sow the seed in early to late summer in rows eighteen to twenty-four inches apart. Sow the seed very thinly in shallow furrows and cover with one-half inch of fine soil. When up and growing, thin to six inches apart. Rutabagas are similar to turnips and may be stored and kept in the same manner.

Sweet Corn

Sweet corn can be raised throughout the country. However, it requires lots of space and is adapted to the larger garden plots. It may be grown in rows with the plants six to eight inches apart or in hills with the hills two and one-half to three feet apart. Either way, rows should be three feet apart. It requires a fertile, well-drained, light soil for best results. It is definitely a warm-weather plant and will not thrive until all danger of frost is past and the ground has begun to warm up. Good cultivation is necessary to ensure that weeds are not stealing nutrients your corn should have.

Just as in other cultivation, a top dressing of fertilizer when the plants are about twelve inches tall will ensure quick growth and good ears. Hilling or mounding soil around the plants when they are about two and one-half to three and one-half feet high will cover any prop roots, retard weed growth, and prove very beneficial to the plants.

Sweet corn should be planted in blocks of four or more rows to ensure good pollination. The hybrid varieties are usually more productive and more resistant to bacterial wilt than the open-pollinated kinds.

Popular yellow hybrids are Illini Xtra-Sweet, Golden Cross Bantam, Marcross, and Ioana. White-grained hybrids are Silver Queen and Country Gentleman.

Potatoes

Potatoes are one of the most productive of all vegetables when grown under favorable conditions. They are a cool-season crop and should be planted as soon in the spring as the ground can be worked. The early varieties include Irish Cobbler, Anoka, Bliss, Norland, and Early Gem. Late varieties include Sebago, Katahdin, Chippewa, Kennebec, and Russet Burbank.

Any fertile, well-drained soil is suitable if properly fertilized. Commercial fertilizers, 5-10-5 or 10-10-10, should be applied at a rate of seven and one-half to fifteen pounds to each one hundred foot row. If manure is used, it must be well-rotted and thoroughly mixed with soil at least a week before planting. The commercial fertilizer must be mixed with the soil in such a manner that the seed pieces will not come in direct contact with it.

When cutting the seed potatoes into pieces for planting, avoid thin or wedge-shaped pieces. Cut the potato into blocky, square-shaped pieces that have at least one eye. It is essential for the seed piece to weigh more than an ounce, inasmuch as the plant will live on this stored, fleshy food while sprouting.

Make furrows about five inches deep, and put a piece of seed potato every twelve to fifteen inches. The furrows should be about two feet apart for the early varieties and about two and one-half to three feet apart for late potatoes. Cover the seed pieces thoroughly to the full depth of the furrow. Usual time for sprouts to appear above ground is about three weeks. Enough seed pieces to plant a one hundred foot row can be cut from about six to eight pounds of seed potatoes. Naturally, the number of pieces will depend on the size of the potato and the number of eyes. The yield from a one hundred foot row can be as low as one bushel or as high as three or more bushels, depending on quality of seed, richness of soil, amount of moisture, climatic conditions, and cultivation.

The potatoes have not attained maximum growth until the tops become withered. At this time, you may dig all the early varieties. After you get them out of the ground, let them stay exposed to the sun for a few hours in order to lose their surface moisture and loose soil. Store them in wooden baskets or crates, or plastic or cardboard containers that have lots of holes so free circulation of air is assured. Cover these containers with newspaper to exclude light. If light strikes the stored potatoes, they will turn green and may become poisonous. The best storage temperature is between about 35° F. and 55° F., avoiding any possibility of freezing. When the storage temperature is too high, the potatoes will sprout.

Late potatoes may be left in the ground four to six weeks after maturing, if the ground is not too wet. Some gardeners leave their early varieties in the ground for quite awhile after the tops wither. Again, it all depends on the temperature and moisture content of the soil. A bit of observation and the digging of a hill or two every two or three days will enable you to keep close check on your tuber crop. At the first sign of deterioration, get them out of the ground and into proper storage.

Handle your potatoes carefully to avoid abrasions and bad spots. Storage for late potatoes is the same as for early varieties, except that you should be extremely careful in the digging, handling, and storage of late potatoes simply because you probably will have them in storage for several months longer than the early varieties.

It is a good idea to plant a small amount of the early variety and a much larger amount of the late variety, which you plan to store and keep for use over a period of several months.

Contrary to popular opinion, potatoes do not have to be put into the ground as soon as it can be worked in the springtime. While it is highly desirable to plant tubers at least two weeks before the date of the last killing frost, let me assure you that planting them around that date, or even as much as two weeks later can result in a good crop. More important than temperature is moisture content of the soil. Prolonged wetness causes the seed to rot instead of coming through the ground. If this happens, your only recourse is to replant—and do not despair, your second planting may give you a bumper crop. If an early planting results in frost damage to sprouts, the plants will usually keep right on growing from parts of the stem unharmed by the frost.

As the tubers multiply and expand in the ground, they quite naturally occupy more and more space. Hence, one must exercise more and more care in cultivation since they also get closer to the surface. A bit of experimentation and observation around one hill of tubers will let you know how close they are to the surface and how far they extend out from the main stem of the plant. At the last good cultivation, the soil should be hoed or plowed in a mound on both sides of the plants to a height of eight to ten inches. On short rows, or small plantings, the soil may be ridged or mounded with the hands after loosening with the hoe.

Sweet Potatoes

Sweet Potatoes are grown throughout most of the country and will succeed in any area that has a frostfree period of about five months accompanied by a relatively high temperature. Sweet potatoes thrive on sandy, warm soils of medium fertility. If the nitrogen content of the soil is too high, you may get lots of vine and not many tubers. Consequently, some growers do not fertilize for sweet potatoes when they follow a crop that was fertilized the year before. If no fertilizer was applied the previous year, apply a fertilizer with a ratio of 2-10-10 (or similar), at the rate of about five pounds to a hundred foot row. For the Northern varieties, the plants are usually set in low ridges about fifteen inches apart with the rows thirty inches apart.

The vines have a great spread, thus virtually eliminating the need for cultivation in the later stages of growth. So cultivate frequently in the early stages and control the weeds. Lifting the vines to prevent rooting at the joints will prolong the period of cultivation, and hand weeding is beneficial. Sweet potatoes withstand dryness easier than most vegetables. Northern varieties of the relatively dry-rooted sort are Jersey Orange, Red Jersey, Nemagold, and Centennial.

Sweet potatoes are grown from "slips" or "draws" that are thrown off from its swollen root. Some call these "slips" sweet potato plants. You can very easily produce your own plants by covering sweet potatoes about two to three inches deep in a box of fertile soil. Keep the soil damp and keep the box in a relatively warm area, such as a basement or heated work area. As the daytime temperatures rise, harden the plants by exposure to outdoor conditions, bringing them back inside at sundown. The plant requires more heat than almost any other vegetable you will grow, so do not plant it outdoors until the soil temperature hits 65° F. You will be pleasantly surprised at the ease with which you can produce your own supply of plants (by selecting one or two big tubers of your favorite variety at the supermarket). And you will be positively astonished at the number of plants that one large tuber will produce when properly handled for slip production.

There is no surface indication as to when the tubers reach maturity. When you think they are big enough to dig, investigate by uncovering a hill. If you are satisfied with their size, proceed with your digging; if not, investigate at a later date. If an early frost arrives, harvest your crop immediately. Frost turns the vines black, and if left in place their juice will pass down into the root and ruin the crop. Unless you can harvest all of a frost-tinged crop immediately, you should cut all vines loose from the roots to prevent further damage. If possible, dig your sweet potatoes on a clear, dry day when the soil is not wet enough to cling to the roots. Do not expose the roots to the sun for more than one or two hours. Then move them to an area where the temperature is 75° F. to 85° F. and spread them out where air can circulate freely around them. This drying or curing process enables the sweet potatoes to lose a lot of moisture and gets them in condition for subsequent storage, preferably at a temperature of 45° F. to 60° F. Extreme care must be exercised in harvesting, handling, curing, and storing of sweet potatoes. No other crop is so susceptible to rot. All cut or injured roots must be used immediately or thrown away. The northern, dry-fleshed varieties are best adapted to areas that are north of the South Carolina border. The best varieties are Red and Yellow Jersey, Nemagold, and Nugget. The moist-fleshed varieties are grown throughout the South and best selections should include Porto Rico,

Yellow Belmont, Nancy Hall, and Goldrush. In the South, sweet potatoes are usually planted two feet apart in the rows, with rows being four or more feet apart, due to luxuriant growth occasioned by high temperatures and extremely favorable growing conditions.

Radishes

The radish is the easiest of all vegetables to raise, and the quickest from seed to table. The earliest varieties, which are small, mild, and quick to mature reach edible size in twenty to thirty days. They include Cherry Belle, French Breakfast, Comet, Scarlet Globe, White Icicle, and Burpee White.

Radishes are grown in many types of soil (as well as window boxes) and are not sensitive as long as the soil is friable, rich, and moist. Fertilize the planting area and sow the seed rather thinly in shallow furrows, covering with one-fourth inch to one-half inch of fine soil. Rows may be as close as eight to twelve inches. Quick growth is the answer to mild, crisp, delicious radishes. They like cold and cool weather and may be sown in the spring as soon as the ground can be worked. Germination usually takes place in four to seven days. Due to their rapid germination and quick growth, radishes are often sparsely sown with carrots and other slower germinating vegetables in order to mark the rows and enable weed control before the other seeds germinate. These radishes are a bonus for seed rows.

For a continuous supply of crisp, mild radishes, one should make additional plantings when the first planting is up and growing well. Short rows of ten feet or less at one planting will usually suffice. After one or two successive plantings you will know just about how long a row you need. Quickly grown radishes are not bothered by insects or plant diseases.

The fall and winter radishes require forty-five to seventy-five days to reach maturity and require cool weather at the end of their growing season. They are more pungent than the early varieties, and are considered a distinct treat. Seeds are sown in July and August for fall and winter use. After attaining good size, some will remain crisp for over a month before harvesting. They may be harvested and stored the same as other root crops. Fall and winter varieties include Long Black Spanish, All Seasons White Radish, China Rose, and Celestial.

When forcing the growth indoors in window boxes or other boxes, one can get quicker, more uniform germination and growth by selecting the largest seeds and rejecting the smaller ones. A mere glance will reveal the great differences in their sizes.

Asparagus

Asparagus is a perennial and one of the earliest spring vegetables. Once the "patch" is established, it requires very little maintenance to remain productive for fifteen or twenty years—some contend for a lifetime. It does best in areas where winter temperatures freeze the surface of the soil.

Asparagus does well on nearly any fertile, well-drained soil. It is a rich feeder and will not produce the quick-growing, tender shoots one is looking for unless properly planted.

In planting, use only one-year old plants or crowns of a variety that is resistant to asparagus rust, such as Mary or Waltham Washington. A fifty-foot row will more than suffice for a family of four. Remove the soil from an area as long as you intend to make the row. Make the trench fifteen inches deep and eighteen inches wide. Fill the bottom of the trench to a depth of six inches with manure, compost, rotted leaves, or peat. Now cover the area with a commercial fertilizer, using five to ten pounds for a fifty-foot row. Cover with about four inches of soil and trample down firmly for good capillary action. Now set the crowns eighteen inches apart and spread the roots well apart. Cover the fleshy roots with two or three inches of fine soil and firm it well. When shoots poke through the soil, cover them again; repeating this covering process until the trench is filled.

Cut none of the stalks the first year. They are needed for growth and nourishment of the crown and roots. In the fall, when the tops turn brown, cut them off at ground level and burn them. Either in the fall, or early in the spring, top dress the row with a generous application of 5-10-5 or similar fertilizer. If manure is used, it must be well-rotted and carefully worked into the soil to avoid injury to the crowns. A modest cutting of shoots may be made during the first six weeks of the second season. Beginning the third year, cut all shoots during the harvesting season. The harvesting should be terminated about July 1 in order for the tops to grow and nourish the crown and roots for production the next year.

As is the case with all vegetables, do not let weeds rob your asparagus of nourishment. Since the tall, wiry bush is rather brittle, cultivation should be frequent and the area kept weed-free until the middle of July. After this, the plants' foliage will fill the row. Obviously, the row or patch of asparagus should be in an area where it will not interfere with annual plowing and gardening.

5
Additional Vegetables for Your Garden

Broccoli

Broccoli—Italian Green Sprouting—is an easily grown, deliciously flavored, vitamin rich vegetable. It may be used fresh, canned, and quick frozen.

Sprouting broccoli is grown in the same way as cabbage. For the earliest crop, sow seeds in flats in the house and transplant the young plants to the garden when the soil has become warm. Seeds sown outdoors in early spring will furnish heads in summer; sowings made in midsummer will provide for a late summer and fall crop. Earliest varieties are ready for the table forty days from planting.

Set plants fifteen inches apart in rows three feet apart. Broccoli grows best during cool weather, but with a little extra care, good results can be obtained even during warm weather. Green Comet, DeCicco, Early Spartan, and Calabrese are among the best known varieties.

Sprouting broccoli with center head and side shoots.

Brussels Sprouts

Brussels sprouts are a member of the cabbage family; they have a more delicate flavor than cabbage. Jade Cross, a true F_1 hybrid, has a wide range of adaptability. Brussels sprouts are a bit hardier than cabbage and will survive the winter outdoors in all the milder, southern sections of the country. They are grown during the same season as early and late cabbage.

The sprouts, or small heads, are formed in the axils of the leaves. Harvest as the small heads begin to crowd, and remove the lower leaves from the stem of the plant to give them more room. The top leaves are required for plant nourishment, so do not disturb them.

Sow the seed thinly in a seedbed any time during the spring up to early June. Transplant the seedlings, as soon as they are large enough to be handled, into another bed and set into rows three feet apart not later than the latter part of July. Brussels sprouts require a light, moist soil and should be cultivated freely. Early June sowings are generally preferred because they will mature into fully developed plants late in the fall.

Cantaloupes (Muskmelons)

There are more than a dozen well-known varieties of cantaloupe. Hale's Best, Hearts of Gold, and Burpee Hydrid are among the best for the home garden.

The most suitable soil for cantaloupes is a rich, warm, sandy loam. Sow the seed after the ground has warmed up, putting eight to ten seeds in groups, allowing two to three inches between seeds and cover with one inch of fine soil. When they are up and growing, thin to two to three plants to a group. The groups should be spaced four to six feet apart each way.

Celery

Celery is a popular vegetable that can be grown in home gardens in most parts of the country at some time during the year. The most common mistake made with celery is failure to allow enough time to grow the plants. Time from transplant to garden to fully mature plants varies from 115 to 135 days, depending on the variety. However, celery may be used from the time plants are one-half or two-thirds grown until fully matured.

Celery seeds are small and slow to germinate. For ease in handling, place the seeds on a small whie cloth and fold and tie the corners together to secure the seeds in the cloth. Soak in tepid water for 24 hours and then distribute them thinly in very shallow trenches in the seed flats or seed bed. Cover them not more than one-half inch with sphagnum moss, leafmold, or some similar material. Keep the seedbed or flat moist until the seed germinates. Moist burlap sacking or plastic covering will help retain moisture in seedbeds and flats. Thin the seedlings to two inches apart each way. Transplant when seedlings are vigorous enough to stand the shock. Set the plants six inches apart in rows that are one and a half to two feet apart. Celery plants are quite delicate when young and a booster solution should be used when they are transplanted. A good booster solution is made by using two tablespoons of 10-10-10 per gallon of water. Use a cup of this solution in the hole where each plant is set.

For successful growth, a rich, moist, but well-drained, friable soil is essential. Prepare the row a week or more before setting the plants. Use abut three pounds of a complete fertilizer for a fifty foot row; and thoroughly mix the fertilizer with the soil.

Burpee's Fordhook, Golden Plume, Green Light, and Giant Pascal are among the better varieties.

Celeriac

Celeriac, or turnip-rooted celery, has been developed for the root instead of the top. It has a flavor similar to celery and is good boiled or in vegetable soup, stews, and other dishes. It may be grated and eaten raw or used in green salads. Its flesh is white and the edible portion is the large, thick root, which may be used when it has grown about two inches across.

They are ready for harvesting about 120 days from planting. The culture is the same as that of celery. Transplant them outdoors when the plants are four to six inches tall. For the fall or main crop, sow in the open ground as early in the spring as the soil can be worked. Transplant the main crop into the permanent rows during July.

Fully grown roots may average four inches in diameter. Roots are easily stored and keep well. For winter use, gather the roots when they are two to four inches in diameter, and store them in a cool, frost proof cellar or similar storage area.

Witloof Chicory (*French Endive*)

Witloof chicory is a choice salad delicacy of mildly acrid flavor for fall and winter. Sow seed in the spring in shallow furrows and cover with not more than one-quarter inch of fine soil. Sow the seed very sparsely and when plants are growing vigorously, thin to stand six inches apart in the rows.

In early fall, cut off foliage one inch above ground level, cover the nubbins with six to eight inches of soil and keep them in place with boards set along the sides. In four to six weeks a pure white blanched stalk should be ready. Cut off about one inch above the top of the root and repeat as above for a second crop, or if chicory is wanted during the winter in cold sections, dig the roots, store them for a few days in a shed or pit so they become thoroughly chilled, then place them upright in boxes and cover with ten inches of sand, light soil, or peat moss. Water and keep them in a warm place indoors. In about a month, the sprouts should break through the surface and be ready for use.

The main use of chicory is for salads during the winter months. The succulent, blanched, tightly folded crowns make one of the most delectable salads known; they are considered a real gourmet treat. They are also delicious when steamed and seasoned. The tender, bleached shoots used in salads are obtained by forcing.* it is best to starting forcing a fresh bunch of roots (removed from storage) at two-week intervals. Each crop can usually be cut three times during the forcing. Roots may be covered only to a depth of three inches and additional covering should be added as sprouts break through. Keep moist and preferably in a temperature range of 50-60° F. Exclude all light.

Collards

A vigorous variety of collards is the Georgia. It grows two to three feet tall and produces a great quantity of large succulent leaves. Collards are grown extensively in the South instead of cabbage, which does not grow well in hot climates.

Collards are easily grown in any rich and moist soil. Sow the seed thinly in drills,[†] three feet apart, early in the spring after all danger of frost has passed. Thin them to avoid overcrowding of the large plants. Cultivate them during the growing season and keep them free of weeds.

They will tolerate light freezing, which improves the mild cabbage-like flavor. Cook whole plants when they are young or strip off the tender rosette or loose cluster of leaves at the top of the fully grown plant.

Garden Cress

Fine curled cress (Burpee's Curlycress) is a valuable "green" to garnish salads and sandwiches. It is ready to eat in just ten days

---

Forcing is the process of inducing a plant to grow faster than normal, or out of regular season. This is done by use of extra heat, light, fertilizer, or moisture.

[†]A *drill* is a small trench for planting seeds. Make the drill immediately before planting to prevent sun-baking and drying out of the soil.

from seeding. It has dark green, finely cut, curled parsley-like leaves. It can be grown all year; outdoors from early spring to fall, indoors during the winter. Sow the seed thinly in rows or broadcast them and cover with not more than one-quarter inch of fine soil. Indoors, curlycress can be grown during the winter in pots or shallow trays placed next to a window. Whether grown indoors or outdoors, successive sowings should be made every two weeks for a continuous supply.

Endive

In the early stages of growth, endive leaves may have a pungent taste, but later the inner leaves blanch and become sweet and tender.

Endive is often grown as a fall crop, although where the summers are seasonably cool it does well from spring sowings. Sow the seed thinly in shallow drills and make successive sowings ten to fourteen days apart. When the young plants are well started, thin them out or transplant them to stand twelve inches apart in the row. When the plants are large and well-formed, draw the leaves together and tie them so that the heart will blanch. For winter use, remove the plants with a ball of earth, place them in a cellar or coldframe where they will not freeze, and tie and blanch them as needed. Green Curled, Salad King, and Broad Leaved Batavian are good varieties. Broadleaved endive is marketed under the name *escarole.*

Garlic

Garlic is a bit more exacting in its cultural requirements than are onions, but it may be grown with a fair degree of success in almost any home garden where good results are obtained with onions. It is not too fussy in its soil requirements and will thrive in any friable, fertile, well-drained soil.

The compound bulbs are composed of eight to twelve cloves. The cloves should be planted root end down about four to six inches apart and covered with an inch of soil firmed around them for good contact. Rows can be short and need not be spaced more than twelve inches apart.

The culture of garlic is the same as that for onions. When

mature, the bulbs are pulled, spread out, and dried in the sun for a few days and then stored in a cool, dry, ventilated area.

By selecting the largest bulbs for seed, you will be assured of having large, well-formed cloves for planting the following season. This selection of the largest and best bulbs for seed will result in a decidedly superior harvest of large, top-quality garlic cloves.

Horse Radish

Horse radish is a perennial that has been grown for centuries to tickle the appetites of those who enjoy hot, peppy, pungent flavors. It is propagated either by crowns or by root cuttings, also called sets. In propagating by crowns, a portion of an old plant, consisting of a piece of foot and crown buds, is separated and planted in a new spot.

Horse radish sets may be obtained from seedsmen—Maliner Kren and New Bohemian are the best known varieties. They are easily grown in any good garden soil that is moist, fertile, deep, and medium heavy.

Plant the sets, which are slender pieces of side roots, in the spring as soon as the soil can be worked. They must be planted with the thick or larger end up, either in an upright or horizontal position, fifteen to eighteen inches apart, in rows two to three feet apart, depending on whether hand or mechanical cultivation is to be used. Set the roots so that their tops will be covered with about two inches of soil. If planted in a horizontal position, it seems best to place the root at an angle: dig a hole long enough to accommodate the root and about three inches deep at one end, slanting to four inches deep at the other; lay the root so that the thick end will be one inch above the smaller end. Cover with two inches of soil, filling in as the plants grow.

Horse radish roots are perfectly hardy and may be planted in the fall or spring. Plants in the home garden can be allowed to grow from year to year, and portions of the roots can be removed as needed. Pieces of roots and crowns remaining in the soil throughout the winter season are usually sufficient to reestablish the plants in the springtime.

Horse radish grows best in the cool fall months and roots dug just before the ground freezes can be stored for long periods in a dark, cool root-cellar. The roots may also be grated or ground to form relish and stored in glass jars. The relish has a comparatively long storage life when kept cool.

Kohlrabi

Kohlrabi is a minor member of the cabbage family. The edible portion is a large bulb produced on the stem above the ground which—if used when young, about two to two and a half inches across—is more delicate than cabbage in both flavor and texture. The crisp, tender flesh has a very mild, sweet, turnip-like flavor. It can be picked and eaten raw or sliced and used in salads. Always cook kohlrabi in its skin to preserve its flavor.

The culture of kohlrabi is similar to that of cabbage and the principal requirements are fertile soil and adequate moisture. Sow in well-prepared and enriched ground as early in the spring as possible. Make a shallow furrow and drop a seed every inch and cover with about 3/4 inch of soil. Firm the soil with your hand or foot, but gently; do not tamp it down. When the plants are four inches tall, thin them or transplant them into very rich soil, setting the plants about a foot apart in the rows. For hand cultivation, rows may be fifteen to eighteen inches apart.

Rapid growth is a must for tender, succulent bulbs. Cultivation should be extremely shallow inasmuch as the young roots spread out just under the surface. A top dressing of 5-10-10 or a similar balanced fertilizer is a good booster for rapid growth. Although they are hardy and able to survive under drought conditions, bulbs subjected to such conditions will be tough and have a strong flavor. The soil must be rich in plant food and always have an adequate supply of moisture in order to ensure rapid growth.

Standard varieties are Early White Vienna and Early Purple Vienna, which mature in fifty-five to sixty days. Harvest them when they are fairly small and pull up the entire plant to avoid disease from rotting roots and leaves. If they are growing faster than you can use them, pick them anyway. Harvest them at the right time, before they get too large, and store them in a cool basement. Kohlrabi may also be stored deep in the soil in straw-lined pits where they will stay crisp and fresh well into the winter.

Okra (Gumbo)

Okra is grown for its edible pods, which have a mucilaginous taste. The immature pods are eaten as a vegetable and they also are used as an herb to flavor soups and stews. The common name of okra is *gumbo*. It is thought of as being strictly a tropical crop; however, it can be grown successfully wherever cucumber and eggplant thrive. It is a tall, rank grower and thrives on heat and any fertile, well-drained soil.

Sow the seed in well-prepared, enriched soil when the ground has warmed up and all danger of frost has passed. Sow the seed about four inches apart in shallow furrows and cover with 1/2 inch of fine soil. Space the rows three feet apart. When the plants are well established, thin the dwarf varieties to stand twelve to eighteen inches apart, and the larger varieties eighteen to thirty inches apart.

Good varieties are Clemson Spineless, Dwarf Green Long Pod, Emerald, and Louisiana Green Velvet. Keep the soil well stirred to avoid crusting and to control the weeds. Pick the pods while they are young and tender. Do not allow any pods to ripen, as ripe pods are unfit for use and soon exhaust the plant.

Peanut

The peanut is an important crop plant that is usually not considered for the home garden. However, throughout the South and Southeast it is grown for home consumption. Peanuts grow well in loose or sandy soil as far north as New York State.

A productive variety, with vines that spread 3-1/2 feet across, is the Jumbo Virginia: the peanuts are extra large and have a rich flavor. They are ready in about 120 days.

For planting, it is not necessary to remove the outer shell. Distribute the peanuts in a furrow two inches deep about the same time corn is planted. Cover the seeds and firm the earth well. Allow eighteen inches between peanuts sown in the row and space the rows thirty-six inches apart.*

When plants are about twelve inches high, mound the soil around the plants as you would mound it around potatoes. This hilling of the soil is extremely important for the production of peanuts. The lower leaves are discarded as the branches grow, and in their place slender stalks appear and force their way into the mounded soil. Peanut pods form on the tips of these stalks, or roots.

*An alternate method of planting is to shell the peanuts and plant two to four of them in groups eighteen inches apart. Why not try both methods and find out from yields which you prefer?

To harvest the crop, dig up the plants just before frost and hang the entire plant, with peanuts on the roots, in a dry, airy building or on poles outside to cure. When the peanuts are well dried, they may be removed from the vines.

Pick out some of the largest and best colored pods for seed to plant next year. These seeds are better than any you can buy for the simple reason that they are adapted to your soil and the local climate.

Roast peanuts in their pods, in an oven preheated to 300° for about twenty minutes. Residual heat will cause the nuts to continue cooking after removal from oven. Therefore, it is best to under-roast. Experiment till you get them exactly the way you want them.

Make your own peanut butter by running the roasted peanuts through the meat grinder until you get the consistency you want.

Popcorn

Popcorn can be ornamental and can provide a pleasant snack for both children and grownups. Popcorn has smaller ears than sweet corn and very hard pointed seeds that explode when heated.

There are several varieties of popcorn with startling differences between them. For example, Black Beauty has jet-black kernels that pop open into bright white, tender popcorn. Burpee's Peppy Hybrid is a deep yellow and pops to white kernels that are large, tasty, and tender. Strawberry Ornamental is a double-purpose popcorn that is highly decorative in flower arrangements and table decorations and is a good eating variety as well. And, there is Calico popcorn with brilliantly colored ears that make fine fall decorations in addition to popping well. The colors run from whites through yellows to blues and dark reds. The Calico variety is a favorite with children around Halloween.

The culture is the same as for sweet corn: SOW IN BLOCKS OF AT LEAST FOUR ROWS SIDE BY SIDE TO INSURE POL-LINATION. Isolate as much as possible from sweet or field corn. The corn should be planted in blocks of at least four rows side by side rather than in a single long row, to insure pollination and development of a full set of kernels. If it is planted near field or sweet corn, cross-pollination will occur and you will not have true popcorn. Instead, you will have a hybridized mixture.

Pull ears after stalks, foliage, and husks are thoroughly dry and hang them in a dry place to cure.

Pumpkin

Pumpkins are easily grown, delicious for pies, and profitable for stock feeding. There is a huge market in both urban and suburban areas throughout the county for pumpkins for Halloween use. However, the gardener is seldom justified in devoting any part of a limited garden area to pumpkins, because many other vegetables give greater returns from the same space.

Hills or groups of pumpkins, containing two plants, should be at least ten feet apart each way. The pumpkin is one of the few vegetables that thrives under partial shade. Therefore, it is a good candidate for intercropping and may be grown among sweet corn or other tall plants. Pumpkin plants should be spaced ten feet in every third or fourth row.

The culture is identical to that of squash. Squash and pumpkins have been hybridized to the extent that their true identity is often in doubt. Good varieties are Big Max, Jack O'Lantern, Connecticut Field, and Small Sugar. Gather and store pumpkins before they are injured by hard frosts. They keep best in a well-ventilated place where temperature ranges between 50 and 60° F.

Cos or Romaine Lettuce

Romaine lettuce is much esteemed for its fresh crispness and sweet flavor. The elongated oval heads have light green outer leaves; the inner leaves are blanched whitish-green. It is distinctive from other lettuce; the head is upright, the leaves are tightly folded, and it is about ten inches tall.

Plant outdoors early to midspring, in rich soil that is well prepared and raked smooth and level. Sow seeds thinly and evenly in rows 1-1/2 feet apart. Cover with 1/2 inch of fine soil. In dry weather, water with a fine spray to keep the surface constantly moist. Gradually thin the plants to six to nine inches apart in the row. Thinnings make delicious, extra-early salads. Several successive sowings in the spring about two weeks apart extend the period of harvest.

For earlier spring harvest, start the seed indoors, in Fertl-Cubes or other starting mediums or soil, six to eight weeks before outdoor planting time. Transplanting outdoors can be done before the last frost date because lettuce is not usually damaged by temperatures as low as 28° F., if the plants have been properly hardened off.

Lettuce grows well in any rich soil but is sensitive to high acidity. A commercial fertilizer with a heavy proportion of phosphorus is recommended.

Soybean

Edible soybeans require twice as long to mature as green or snap beans. Soil and cultural requirements and methods of growing are essentially the same as for bush snap beans. Kanrich and Giant Green are the most widely grown varieties.

For use as a green vegetable, soybean pods should be harvested when the seeds are fully grown but before the pods turn yellow. The green beans are difficult to remove from the pods, but if the pods are boiled for about five minutes, they can be easily shelled.

The yields per unit area of land are about the same as are usually obtained with peas and are thus less than can be obtained with many other vegetables. When one considers the long growing season, the yield, and the difficulty in processing—only those with large gardens who seek variety should bother to grow edible soybeans.

Spinach

Tampala or Fordhook spinach thrives during long, hot summer days. The plants make delicious "greens," either raw as a salad or cooked like spinach. It may be canned or frozen and is a decidedly superior green.

Sow seed thinly after all danger of frost is past and the ground is warm; cover with 1/4 inch of fine soil. Space rows twelve to fifteen inches apart. For a continuous supply of young greens, make several sowings about two weeks apart. Within six to eight weeks from sowing, Fordhook spinach is five or six inches high and is ready to use.

However, if you wish to grow plants to maturity, space the rows two feet apart and thin the plants to stand two feet apart in the row. Tips four to five inches long may be cut from the ends of branches of larger plants and, unless too many are cut at one time, new growth will provide continuous cuttings throughout the season.

Sunflowers

Sunflowers make beautiful plants for use as backgrounds or screens because of their stately growth. You can grow your own song bird and poultry food while enjoying these gorgeous, stately plants.

There are many varieties with seed heads ranging from three to twelve inches in diameter. Heights of the plants vary from three to twelve feet. A popular three-foot variety is Teddy Bear. A prodigious, stately nine- to twelve-footer is the Giant Sunflower, which is a perennial.

Sunflowers are easy to grow and thrive in almost any soil exposed to sun. Sow the seeds of annuals in the spring and divide the perennials.* Follow planting instructions on seed packets for best results.

Watermelon

You may have your choice of round, oval, or long watermelons, ranging in weight from six to forty pounds. The time from seed to melon varies from seventy to ninety days, depending on the variety planted.

Watermelons like rich, rather sandy soil, well cultivated, with lots of moisture. Mixing two bucketsful of well-rotted manure or composted material with the soil in each hill will materially assist the watermelon crop. It is a good idea to boost the available plant food by also mixing one-half pound of a balanced fertilizer with the soil in each hill.

Plant in well-worked and fertilized ground after all danger from frost is past and the ground is warm and dry. Plant about ten seeds in a hill in a ring about one foot across. Cover the seeds with about one inch of soil and press the soil down gently to assist germination. Hills should be spaced eight feet apart. When plants are well established, thin to about three plants to the hill, leaving the hardiest. Keep weeds under control until vines cover intervening space.

Charleston Gray is one of the newer watermelons that is highly recommended because it combines fine eating quality with excellent keeping and shipping qualities. It is resistant to fusarium wilt, anthracnose, and sunburn.† Other popular varieties are New Hampshire Midget, Kleckley's Sweet Improved, and Burpee Hybrid Seedless.

---

*The roots of perennials are easily divided after the soil is carefully removed. Each section of a divided root can be replanted to produce a new plant.

†Anthracnose is a destructive disease, caused by fungi, which attacks the grape, cotton, bean, melon, and other plants.

Due to the large space requirements, only gardeners with lots of garden area can afford to grow watermelon.

Strawberries

Strawberries are grown successfully in every state. They are easy to grow and beginners are proud of their fine berries.*

BEARING

Standard varieties set in the spring of one year will bear their best crop in May or June of the next year. Everbearing varieties set in the spring produce berries in late summer and fall of the same year.

PLANTING

Early spring planting is of the greatest importance in growing strawberries. This means just as early in the spring as weather permits preparation of the land. If the plants are established while the soil is still cool and moist, a good stand results. If the plants are dormant and there is good irrigation, later setting is possible but it is not as easy. Planting time is usually February, March, and early April in the southern states; March and April in the middle states; April and May in the northern states.

PLANTING DISTANCES

In general, we recommend setting plants eighteen to twenty inches apart in rows four feet apart. This requires a little over 7,000 plants per acre (see table). Somewhat closer planting is satisfactory in small gardens where space is limited, or for the hill system (as with everbearers), or for late setting where a good stand is uncertain.

For the small garden, order seven plants for each ten feet of row you want to set or plan on one plant for each five square feet. Thus, for a plot ten by ten feet, you would need about twenty plants.

PLANTING DISTANCES

In general, we recommend setting plants eighteen to twenty inches apart in rows four feet apart. This requires a little over 7,000

---

*This section on strawberries courtesy of W. F. Allen Company.

PLANTS FOR VARIOUS PLANTING DISTANCE

Rows (distance apart)	In the row (inches)	Total plants per acre
3 ft.	18	9,680
3 ft.	24	7,260
3½ ft.	18	8,297
3½ ft.	24	6,223
4 ft.	18	7,260
4 ft.	24	5,445
3-2/3 ft.	18	7,128

plants per acre (see table). Somewhat closer planting is satisfactory in small gardens where space is limited, or for the hill system (as with everbearers), or for late setting where a good stand is uncertain.

For the small garden, order seven plants for each ten feet or row you want to set or plan on one plant for each five square feet. Thus, for a plot ten by ten feet, you would need about twenty plants.

SOIL AND LOCATION

Any soil that makes good yields of garden or field crops will produce strawberries in abundance, whether that soil is a light sandy loam or a heavy clay. Here are some pointers.
1. In rolling country a sloping field gives better air drainage and less injurious frosts.
2. Run the berry rows across a steeply sloping field rather than up and down to help prevent erosion.
3. Follow a hoed crop to make less weeds and grass for the strawberries to contend with.
4. Avoid sod land that may harbor grub worms that will cut or injure your plants. Treatment for grub worms makes the use of sod land much safer.
5. Change the place of the strawberry bed every few years. It will help to keep up the vigor and growth and reduce the danger of a buildup of disease and insect trouble.
7. Most important of all—select land that holds moisture well because (a) it is naturally springy, (b) it has a high water table (c) lots of organic matter in the form of animal manures or green crops has been incorporated in the soil. Of course, if irrigation is available, you can give the plants water when necessary.

IRRIGATION

It would be most worthwhile to use irrigation for strawberries—for establishing the new bed, as well as at fruiting time. Irrigation is not mandatory, but if you have a frost during bloom, irrigation during the danger hours can save strawberry crops from frost and freeze damage with temperatures as low as 20° F.

LAND PREPARATION

In late winter or very early spring the land should be plowed or spaded to a depth of six to eight inches. Then it should be leveled off with a harrow or rake to form a smooth friable planting bed. Following are some hints that will help you to produce bigger, better crops of berries.

1. In late summer plow under a heavy growth of green crops such as peas, beans, clover, sowed corn, weeds, grass, etc. All of these rot quickly and are much more valuable for the strawberry crop if plowed under while still green.
2. An early fall sowing of rye or wheat will give a heavy sod that can be plowed under in late winter or very early spring. This will be easier to handle if disced up thoroughly before plowed.*
3. Apply horse, cow, hog, or sheep manure at the rate of five to twenty tons per acre. This is the best of all preparations for a fine crop of berries. Results are almost equally good if one of these applications has been made for the previous crop. For small areas a good guide in the application of manure is to figure on one to two bushels for every one hundred square feet.

PUTTING PLANTS IN GROUND

Any method of planting that leaves the roots reasonably straight down in the soil is good. The roots should be spread with the soil pressed tightly against them and the bud just at the surface. With plants that have very long roots, clip them off to about four or five inches; this will not hurt the plants and will make a good job of setting easier. No matter how long or how short the leaf stems, fruit stems, or roots may be at the time of setting, the bud must be just at the surface.

Disced is the same as *disked*. The reference here is to the use of a disk harrow—a harrow with sharp disks that can revolve, used to break up the soil for sowing. Also, some harrows have "fixed" disks that do not revolve. A disk is a thin circular plate.

A good garden trowel is the best setting tool for work in small plots; in larger fields it is common practice to use a transplanter. With a transplanter it is very important that the setting depth of the plants be checked behind the planter.

CHEMICAL FERTILIZER

On very fertile soils no chemical fertilizer is needed. Have a soil test made and follow the recommendation of your local supplier or county agent.

LIME

If other crops, weeds, or grass have made a good growth on the land you have selected for strawberries, it does not need lime.

A pH range of 5.7 to 6 is best; 5 to 7 is satisfactory if the organic matter content of the soil is fairly high.

CARE OF PLANTS

Plants should be set as soon as you get them, if possible. Dip the roots in water and keep them protected when you take them to the garden or field for setting. A hot day is bad for setting strawberry plants. A hot windy day is terrible. A cool cloudy day is fine. If plants must be kept a while, small lots can be kept in the family refrigerator. The very best way to hold plants is in cold storage between 29 and 32° . Never, never put plants in a freezer where temperatures will go below 28° .

CULTIVATING, HOEING AND TRAINING

Shallow cultivating and hoeing (not to exceed two inches) kills weeds, conserves moisture, and enables new runners to take root.

Uncover the buds; failure to do this will give you a poor stand.

Most of the training of new runners is done at hoeing time. Train the first strong new runners out like spokes from a wheel and root them until a fruiting row 1-1/2 to 2-1/2 feet wide has been formed. Four to eight plants per square foot of fruiting bed is enough; when ever possible later runners should be cut off.

MULCHES

Mulching is necessary for winter protection in all the northern states and would be helpful in many fields as far south as Virginia and Kentucky. In addition to giving protection from cold, mulching helps to keep down weeds and grass, to conserve soil moisture, and to keep the fruit bright and clean.

The mulch should be applied in the fall after frost and light freeze (25 to 28° F.) have occurred but before hard freezing (20° F. or lower). It should be removed, at least partly, soon after growth starts in the spring.

Wheat straw and marsh grass are considered the best materials. Rye straw, pine needles, coarse strawy manure, buckwheat hulls, and various kinds of hay are satisfactory. In some sections, sawdust has been used with good results. Use whatever you have or can buy at a reasonable price.

Types of Plants

EARLY VARIETIES

EARLIBELLE—*Vigor and Beauty*

Plants: Small but great for producing runners. Productive. Adapted from Virginia south.

Berries: Medium to large. Bright red. Glossy and firm. Slightly tart.

Something Special: Earlibelle is outstanding for firmness, toughness, flesh and skin color in freezing and canning.

SUNRISE—*The Good Grower*

Plants: Very vigorous. Good producers of fine berries. Excellent resistance to disease. Grow well even in dry weather.

Berries: Conic. Medium to large. Firm, light, bright red and attractive.

Something Special: High flavor makes the Sunrise delicious for table use. A little light in color for best freezing. Great for shipping.

MID-SEASON VARIETIES

CATSKILL—*The Leader*

Plants: Widely adapted. Very productive. Make runners freely. Vigorous grower. Hardy. Resistant to verticillium wilt.

Berries: Very large. Long conic. Not too firm. Bright crimson skin, light red flesh. Mildly sub-acid.

Something Special: Good for desserts. Excellent for freezing. Loaded with Vitamin C.

SURECROP—*For Sure Crops*

Plants: Widely adapted, upper south to north. Large size. Vigorous producer. Free in runner production under most conditions. One of the very best for resistance to diseases of plant or foliage. Drought resistant.

Berries: Large. Round conic. Irregular. Firm. Glossy. Medium red skin. Light red flesh. Tart.

Something Special: Fine for desserts. Excellent for freezing.

LATE VARIETIES

ALBRITTON—*The One with Class*

Plants: Vigorous. Make runners freely. High yields in North Carolina and parts of Virginia.

Berries: Large. Uniform. Conic. Very firm. Glossy, bright red skin. Solid red flesh. Excellent flavor.

Something Special: Beautiful berries. Easy to sell. Excellent for shipping and freezing.

JERSEYBELLE—*The "Belle" of Berries*

Plants: Large. Good runner makers. Productive from southern New Jersey northward. Susceptible to leaf diseases, red stele and verticillium wilt.

Berries: Large. Showy. Glossy. Medium red. Blunt conic. Tender skin. Prominent seeds.

Something Special: Size and beauty make Jerseybelle great for local markets and pick-your-own. Not too good for freezing.

EVERBEARING VARIETIES

GEM (SUPERFECTION)—*Old Favorite*

Plants: Hardy. Good producer. Drought susceptible.

Berries: Light red. Irregular. Tart. Medium firm.

Something Special: Attractive berries for table use or local market.

OZARK BEAUTY—*Good Eating*

Plants: Good runner production. Good yielder.

Berries: Large, Sweet. Good flavor. Firm

Something Special: Pretty plants and good yields from June until first frost. Good freezer.

The idea of growing strawberries in barrels appeals to those who love growing plants but have only limited space. These barrels are pretty enough for use anywhere in the house and they will be an added attraction to the patio or garden. Watch the plants grow and bloom; enjoy their beauty and life; and then, glory be, harvest some delicious strawberries for your table.

Order twenty-five plants for your barrel from our list of many varieties. When you receive your barrel, fill it with good rich soil and set the plants in the holes already bored for them, with a few left to fill the top.

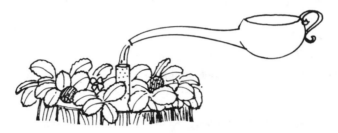

For easier watering—when the barrel is one-third full of soil, place on end in the center of the barrel a one or two inch tile, plastic or metal pipe or wooden channel long enough to extended up even with the surface. The tube should have holes all around, and up and down to allow for circulation of air and water. Just water through this center pipe to give the lowest plants the moisture they need.

Courtesy of W.F. Allen Company

Buy A Barrel of Joy

Order a Berry Barrel now—for yourself, a dear relative or friend. A wonderful gift—one that will be cherished for years.

For $10.00 we will deliver to your home (or another address, if requested), insured, with all transportation charges paid, this beautiful barrel. Standing 12 inches high and 10 inches across, banded in brass, it is indeed·a little beauty. Pretty enough for the living room and lovely for the patio, it will hold 25 plants and the green of the foliage is most attractive against the stained rubbed pine of the barrel.

BUY ONE for yourself, watch the plants grow, bloom and produce fruit.

BUY ONE for a dear friend or relative and give many happy hours of pleasure.

Courtesy of W.F. Allen Company

117

6

Herbs

Herbs

Herbs add a gourmet touch to food that not only improves the flavor but also appeals to our senses of sight and smell in a most tantalizing manner.

It is no culinary secret that soup stock, butter, eggs, milk, and cheese quickly absorb the herb flavoring. To achieve maximum flavor, mix the herbs with one of these ingredients and let stand for a few hours before using. A bit of practice coupled with critical sampling will soon enable you to add the gourmet touch to most any food.

While there are more than sixty well-known and popular herbs used throughout the country, you can revolutionize both your garden and your culinary skills with only a few of them. The following are recommended for their ornamental and aesthetic

119

values as well as culinary use: anise, borage, caraway, chives, dill, florence, fennel, parsley, peppermint, rosemary, sage, spearmint, sweet basil, sweet majoram, summer savory, and thyme.

Herbs do well in any ordinary well-drained soil; a good supply of four varieties can be grown on a border strip of garden that is only twenty feet long and four feet wide. Herbs require no more attention than other garden plants and the results can be most rewarding from an ornamental as well as a practical point of view.

Herb	Planting	Description	Uses	Harvest
Anise (*Pimpinella anisum*)	Full sun; well-drained loam. Soak seed 24 hrs. in tepid water. Thin as required.	Annual, 2 ft., graceful plant with small white flowers and straw-colored seed. Quite potent.	Green leaves in salads, soups, stews, and for garnish. Seeds in cakes and cookies. Oil in liquers, medicines, and perfumes.	Cut green leaves as needed. When seeds turn grayish clip umbels and dry in cool, airy location. Store
Borage (*Borago officinalis*)	Full sun; dry, well-drained soil. Easily transplanted.	Annual 1½ ft., star-shaped blue flowers.	Excellent bee forage. Good for cut flowers. Leaves minced and used in teas and salads.	Cut young leaves any time. Cut flowers anytime.
Caraway (*Carum carui*)	Full sun; dry, friable soil. Hardy, but slow in germination.	Biennial, 1½-2 ft. lacey, creamy, yellow flowers. Dark brown seeds with lighter-colored ridges.	Green leaves in stews, soups, salads. Seeds in cakes, bread, sauerkraut, and cheeses. Oil in liquers, medicine and for perfumes.	Cut seed heads when no longer green and dry in cool, airy location. Store in glass jars.

121

Herb	Planting	Description	Uses	Harvest
Chives (*Allium schoenprasum*)	Spring or fall, indoors or outdoors. Seed or divisions. Full	Perennial with onion-like tops. Lavender flowers. Vigorous and grows in thick clumps.	Flavor salads, soups, omelets, cheeses, and appetizers.	Cut leaves as needed about 2 inches above bulblets.
Dill (*Anethum graveolens*)	Early spring in average garden soil after it is warm. Full sun. Thin or transplant to stand 1 ft. apart in the row.	Annual, 2-3 ft. Threadlike foliage and greenish-yellow flowers. Young tender green shoots used for flavoring.	Leaves and shoots used in fish sauces, potato salad, and cottage cheese. Dried dill weed condiment in soups, stews, and omelets. Seeds for pickling, vinegars, and condiment.	Cut when seeds are ripe; hang whole sprays up to dry. Store in glass jars.
Florence Fennel or Finocchio (*Foeniculum dulce*)	Early spring in rich well-prepared soil. Thin to stand 10 inches apart in the row. Plants should be earthed up when half-grown and treated like celery.	Rapidly growing annual, 2½ ft., with feathery foilage and enlarged leaf bases.	Both foliage and seed are used for flavoring food. Enlarged, blanched leaf bases are boiled or eaten raw like celery. Anise-like flowers.	Cut when blanched leaf bases are mature and when seeds are mature.

122

Herb	Planting	Description	Uses	Harvest
Parsley (*Petroselinum crispum*)	Soak seeds in tepid water 48 hrs. Rich, moist soil, in full sun. Can thrive in partial shade	Compact biennial grown as annual. 8-12 inches tall. Finely cut and curled leaves.	For garnish and flavor in meats, soups, salads, omelets. Parsley soup is delicious.	Cut fresh leaves and sprigs as needed. Cut and dry in fall and store in glass jars.
Peppermint (*Mentha piperita*)	Early spring by runners and stolons. Also propagated by slips and branches in moist sand.	Perennial, 2-3 ft. Vigorous in wet, favorable locations. Long narrow leaves, Flowers usually purple. Reddish undertone throughout plant.	Either fresh or dried leaves in teas, beverages, and jellies. Peppermint oil is used in medicines and to flavor many toiletries.	Cut fresh leaves as needed. For drying, cut stems when flowers start to bloom. Dry in shade and store in glass jars.
Rosemary (*Rosmarinus officinalis*)	Start seeds indoors and transplant in sunny, dry, well-drained soil in a sheltered location.	Perennial, 2-4 ft. Blue flowers. Leaves are evergreen, without stalks and are very fragrant.	Tender tips and buds used to flavor meats, sauces, soups, seafood, and poultry.	Cut fresh leaves any time. For drying, gather as plants flower and dry in shade. Store in glass jars.

123

Herb	Planting	Description	Uses	Harvest
Sage (Salvia officinalis)	Seed or cuttings in good well-drained garden soil in full sun.	Perennial, 1-2 ft. Light, woolly, wrinkled leaves. White, blue, or purple flowers.	Use dried in poultry stuffings and sausages. Flavors pork, veal, and cheeses. Sage is strong and should be used sparingly.	Cut sparingly first year. Tender tips and buds have most flavor. Strip leaves from stem and dry in shade. Store in glass jars.
Spearmint (Mentha spicata)	Early spring by runners and stolons. Also propagated by slips and branches in moist sand.	Perennial, 2-3 ft. Vigorous in wet, favorable locations. Dark green, smooth, graceful plant with tiny, white flowers with purple markings.	Fresh leaves are minced to garnish and flavor peas and glazed carrots. Used in mint sauce and cold beverages. Use fresh and dried in teas and jellies.	Cut fresh leaves as needed. Cut stems when flowers start to bloom and dry in shade. Store in glass jars.
Sweet Basil (Ocimum basilicum)	Full sun; well-drained garden soil. Easily grown in warm soil.	Compact annual 1-1½ ft. tall. Pinch center bud out when seedling is 6 inches high to make more compact bush.	The flavor is flower-like and goes well with a wide variety of cooked foods. One of best of seasoning herbs.	Cut leaves soon as plants are large enough to stand the operation. When flowers begin to open, cut leaves for drying and storage.

124

Herb	Planting	Description	Uses	Harvest
Sweet Marjoram *(Origanum marjoram)*	Full sun in dry, well-drained garden soil. May be started indoors and transplanted when garden soil is warm.	Annual, 1-2 ft. Very fragrant and aromatic. Tiny, gray-green leaves covered with down.	Season sausages and poultry stuffings. Use mixed in salads or as garnish. Good in most cooked foods.	Cut fresh leaves as needed. When flowers start to appear, cut leaves and flowering tops, strip leaves, dry in shade and store in glass jars.
Summer Savory *(Satureia hortensis)*	Sunny location in well-prepared, good garden soil. Also by division of root-stocks or cuttings.	Annual, 1-1½ ft. Long and narrow lance-shaped leaves. Pink to purplish small flowers.	Use fresh leaves in peas and snap beans or for garnish. Use dried leaves in sausages, meats, and poultry dressings.	Cut fresh leaves sparingly as needed. Gather plants when in full bloom, dry foliage thoroughly in shade and store in glass jars.
Thyme *(Thymus vulgaris)*	Full sun in rather poor soil containing plenty of lime. Plants enjoy nestling against warm stones and do well in rock gardens, alongside stone walks and on sunny banks.	Perennial, 6-12 in. tall. Grayish, tiny evergreen leaves. Small lilac to purplish flowers. This attractive plant improves the appearance of any garden or walkway.	Used to flavor wines, seafood, sauces, soups, stuffings and salads. Oil of thyme is used to perfume toiletries.	Cut fresh leaves as needed. For winter use cut the stems before flowers appear and dry in an airy and shady place. Store in glass jars.

125

7

Gardening Hints

1. All vegetable plants need good soil, enough water, enough sunlight, adequate spacing between plants, and proper temperature range for steady, vigorous growth.
2. For good sustained yield of top-quality vegetables over a long bearing season, the plants will require a continuous supply of nutrients. Weeds must be kept to a minimum so they do not steal the plant food and shade the plants.
3. Assuming that different varieties are planted during their proper season, the gardener can control or improve all of the plants' requirements, except the amount of sunlight they get.
4. If you dislike using an insecticide for bug control; you may want to "plant" some praying mantises and ladybugs in your garden.

127

Both of these beneficial insects can be obtained from Burpee and Gurney. Encourage songbirds to stay near your garden by providing a bath and year-round feeding. Birds consume millions of insects.

5. Apply a complete, balanced fertilizer to the garden soil before sowing seeds or setting out plants. When plants are half-grown make a second application in the form of top dressing.

6. The garden needs about an average of one inch of rainfall per week. When this does not occur, you must provide the water. In very dry weather, water the garden thoroughly to a depth of several inches about once a week.

7. Cultivate the soil very shallowly, 1-2 inches, as soon as soil is workable after each good rainfall. This gardening practice destroys weeds, creates a dust mulch for retention of moisture, and keeps the soil receptive for the next rainfall.

8. Excessively heavy rainfall during the bearing season of vegetable crops tends to leach plant nutrients out of the soil. Replace these much-needed plant foods with a judicious application of top dressing, using a balanced fertilizer, compost, or well-rotted cow manure.

9. Plants yielding an abundance of fruits over a long bearing season benefit enormously from two or three well-spaced top dressings. Just remember to top dress sparingly, keep fertilizer off foliage and roots, and cultivate or rake it into the soil.

10. Do not make the mistake of trying to compare the nutrient requirements of a vegetable garden with those of field crops. Field crops, such as soybeans and corn, are "one-shot" affairs: that is, they bear only once, whereas, a lot of vegetable plants continue to bear and grow repeated yields of their fruits over a period of two or three months. Obviously, their nutrient requirements are much higher than those of field crops.

11. Mounding or hilling the soil with the hands, around the stems of half-grown green beans, has a very salubrious effect. It keeps the roots cooler, increases aeration of the soil, retains more moisture, helps control weeds, and keeps the plants from falling over. Young squash, tomato, pepper, eggplant, and cucumber plants and vines also benefit from this same treatment. Merely move the soil into place, leave it loose, do not pat or firm it down.

12. Newly transplanted seedlings cannot take the blistering heat of an extremely hot day nor the effects of a strong wind. You may have to shade and protect them with inverted baskets or cardboard boxes with holes cut in the sides for ventilation for 2 or 3 days.

13. Start a compost pile with green grass clippings, topsoil, and a sprinkling of a balanced fertilizer. Gradually add garden refuse, pea and bean vines, leaves, and more topsoil as these materials become available. Plan on keeping a compost pile working for you all the time.

14. The real secret to growing fine lettuce plants is rapid growth and no crowding in the row. Rapid growth demands an abundance of plant nutrients and plenty of moisture. Fertilize, compost, and get the seedbed well prepared before sowing. Make adequate preparation and quality and quantity of harvest will be pleasing.

15. Garbage from the kitchen is rich in nitrogen and other plant nutrients. Bury the garbage, spread out a bit, in a garden area for direct soil building and enrichment. It must be deep enough to avoid detection by stray animals. Add layers to the compost pile; covering with straw, grass clippings, leaves, or topsoil. Kitchen garbage is an excellent activator for the compost pile.

16. You are urged to give gardening a "one hundred percent" try for one full season. The outdoor exercise tones the muscles, relaxes the mind, and stimulates the appetite. Gardening affords an invigorating contrast to the oftentimes impersonal work some of us do at our regular jobs. A successful first season will make you fall in love with gardening.

17. *Succession of crops.* All garden space should be kept fully occupied throughout the growing season. In arranging the garden, all early maturing crops should be grouped so that as soon as one crop is harvested another takes its place. For example, early peas or beans can very properly be followed by late cabbage, celery, carrots, or beets; early sweet corn or potatoes can be followed by kale, spinach, or turnips.

18. *Intercropping.* It is not always necessary to wait until the early crop is entirely removed. A later crop may be planted between rows of potatoes. As a general rule, crops subject to attack by the same diseases and insects should not follow each other.

19. *Saving the late tomatoes.* Even up to first frost there will be

green tomatoes on the vines. Before the frosts come, pick all the tomatoes and wrap them individually in about three layers of newspaper. Store them three or four layers deep in open crates or boxes. Boxes may be kept in any warm area and tomatoes will ripen without aid of light in two to four weeks, depending on temperature and condition of tomatoes when wrapped. A surplus of smaller green tomatoes could be used for relishes, pickling, etc.

20. *Hybrid seed and hybrid plants.* It's a well-established fact that hybrid vegetable plants are more disease-resistant and yield more uniform fruits over a longer season than comparable standard varieties. Consequently, the extra cost is entirely justifiable, and competent, experienced gardeners prefer the hybrids.

21. *Harvesting.* It is mandatory that you keep all cucumbers, squash, peppers, eggplant, peas, beans, etc. picked as they reach maturity. If fruits are left on plants and vines till seeds inside them reach full maturity and ripen, the plants and vines will show a marked decrease in production. In some instances, they will stop bearing completely.

22. *Hills versus groups.* Most of us have grown up with the idea of hills of squash, hills of cucumbers, etc. And many gardeners actually draw soil up into a hill or mound to plant these vegetables. However, this is not good gardening practice, simply because a hill or mound of soil loses its moisture content much faster than soil that is level with the surface of the earth. Accordingly, let's talk about *groups* of squash, *groups* of cucumbers, etc. Do not mound or draw up the soil into a hill; instead, prepare the soil for planting on the level surface.

23. Take full advantage of the expertise of your county extension and agricultural agents on all facets of vegetable gardening. These people are extremely knowledgeable and enjoy being of assistance.

24. Prevent or control most plant diseases by growing disease-resistant varieties, by keeping garden refuse cleaned up, by removing and burning "sick" plants, and by planting the same variety in a different location each year.

25. Send for seed catalogs in January to allow ample time for planning the early garden. If animal pests are likely to be a

nuisance, send for literature about *Havahart*® traps. Obtain your strawberry plants from specialists who handle only the best.

26. Control harmful insects by using one of the excellent all-purpose sprays or dusts on the market. Examine your plants carefully and either hand pick the bugs or spray or dust at first signs of insect infestation.

27. *Feeding seedlings in a sterile medium.* Make a liquid fertilizer by dissolving one tablespoon of 10-10-10 in a gallon of water. Or, use two tablespoons of 5-10-5 to a gallon of water. This fertilizer may be applied to the seedlings at 5- to 7-day intervals.

28. When leaves of herbs are continually being cut or picked for fresh use the plant is hard put to maintain its vigor. Top dressing with a complete fertilizer, or the use of a liquid fertilizer, at 3- or 4-week intervals will enable the plant to remain healthy and productive.

29. *Pollination of sweet corn.* Sweet corn pollination is best achieved by planting the corn in blocks. For example, four 25-foot rows are far superior to one 100-foot row. Sweet corn tends to cross-pollinate with field corn. So, if you have a choice, do not plant sweet corn adjacent to field corn.

30. Did you ever stop and think about the enormous amount of time and energy expended on lawns—which are primarily for decorative purposes. If you put this same amount of time and energy into the growing of snap beans, tomatoes, and squash, you would be positively astonished at the savings on your grocery bill.

31. Vegetable plants faithfully reflect the fertility of the soil in which they are grown. Soils that are deficient in organic matter and low in nutrients will not produce top-quality vegetables.

32. Keep a record of your gardening activities. Your specific knowledge about successful gardening will expand quite rapidly if you take the time to keep a brief record of your activities. Record varieties and planting dates—time to first fruit and length of bearing season. This may seem like a lot of extra work, but you can record four hours of gardening activity in about five minutes of writing. Good records enable you to plan a better, more productive garden for the coming year. In two short growing seasons you will become a successful, experienced gardener.

Appendix A

Weights and Measures

Bushel of Apples	48-50 pounds
Bushel of Barley	48 pounds
Bushel of Beans	60 pounds
Bushel of Beets	56-60 pounds
Bushel of Buckwheat	42-52 pounds
Bushel of Corn (in the ear, husked)	70 pounds
Bushel of Corn (shelled)	56 pounds
Bushel of Cornmeal	48 pounds
Bushel of Oats	32 pounds
Bushel of Onions	52-56 pounds
Bushel of Peas	60 pounds
Bushel of Potatoes	60 pounds
Bushel of Turnips	55-60 pounds
Bushel of Wheat	60 pounds
Pint of water	1.046 pounds
Gallon of water	8.34 pounds
Cubic foot of water	62.42 pounds

LAND MEASURE

300 feet by 145.2 feet	1 acre
220 feet by 198 feet	1 acre
110 feet by 396 feet	1 acre
100 feet by 200 feet	½ acre approximately
50 feet by 100 feet	1/8 acre approximately
33 feet by 66 feet	1/20 acre exactly

An acre contains 43,560 square feet and is almost exactly 209 by 209 feet. There are 640 acres in a square mile.

DRY MEASURE (LEVEL FULL)
(Used in measuring dry materials)

3 teaspoons equal 1 tablespoon
16 teaspoons equal 1 cup
2 cups equal 1 pint
2 pints equal 1 quart
4 quarts equal 1 gallon
2 gallons equal 1 peck
4 pecks equal 1 bushel

FLUID MEASURES

40-50 drops equal 1 teaspoon
3 teaspoons equal 1 tablespoon
2 tablespoons equal 1 ounce
8 ounces equal 1 cup
2 cups equal 1 pint
2 pints equal 1 quart
4 quarts equal 1 gallon

Appendix B

Fertilizers

How to calculate small measures of fertilizers from recommended applications by weight for large areas.

Books and bulletins on agriculture and gardening usually give recommendatins for the use of fertilizers and lime in tons or pounds per acre, or in pounds per thousand or hundred square feet. The gardener often finds it difficult to convert these weights into the measures needed for a small plot or for a single row or a single plant; Tables 1 and 2 make the conversions for him, using the common household measurements of pints, cups, tablespoons, and teaspoons.

For example, if 300 pounds of superphosphate or mixed fertiizer are recommended per acre, you will find by turning to table 1 that this means 7 pounds per thousand square feet or 11 ounces (1½ cups) per hundred square feet. Then, turning to table 2, you will find that 2 cups per hundred square feet means ½ cup for each

10-foot row if the rows are 3 feet apart, or 6 tablespoons full for each plant if the plants are spaced 5 x 5 feet. A large number of such conversions are given for various kinds of fertilizer material and to fit various needs.

The rates to be selected for the various fertilizing materials depend on the soil and its previous treatments and the requirements of the plants. Certain materials—ground limestone, where needed, and superphosphate—are used in relatively large quantities; other materials, such as borax, are used sparingly. For example, small supplemental additions of ammonium nitrate can be beneficial to tomatoes, whereas large quantities would injure the plants.

The values tabulated are near enough for all practical purposes, though they are only approximate, since the weight of a given volume of a material will vary with its moisture content and texture. The standard pint, cup, tablespoon (tbs.), and teaspoon (tsp.) are used for liquid measure. Level-full measures are used.*

It will be useful to remember: (1) that a pint of water weighs just a little more than a pound (actually, 1.046 pounds); (2) that an acre is equivalent to 43,560 square feet (a plot about 209 feet square); and (3) that a pint is equivalent to 2 cups, or 32 tablespoons, or 96 teaspoons.

---

*For materials not included in the lists, carefully weigh a full pint and determine approximately the group to which it belongs.

TABLE 1

WEIGHTS OF VARIOUS FERTILIZING MATERIALS PER ACRE, PER 1,000 SQUARE FEET, PER 100 SQUARE FEET, AND THE APPROXIMATE EQUIVALENT-VOLUME MEASURES FOR 100 SQUARE FEET, GROUPED ACCORDING TO WEIGHT.

Materials	Weights specified per -			Volume Measure for 100 Sq. Ft.
	Acre	1,000 Sq. Ft.	100 Sq. Ft.	
Weight about the same	Pounds	Pounds	Pounds	Pints
as that of water	1,300	30	3	3
Examples: ammonium	870	20	2	2
nitrate, ammonium	435	10	1	1
sulfate, potassium				Cups
chloride, sodium	220	5	½	1
nitrate.	110	2½	¼	½
				Pints
Weight about 1 $3/10$	5,660	130	13	10
that of water	3,485	80	8	6
Examples: ground	870	20	2	1½
limestone, ground			Ounces	
dolomitic limestone,	565	13	21	1
potassium sulfate.				Cups
	280	6½	11	1
			Pounds	Pints
Weight about $9/10$	1,960	45	4½	5
that of water	1,650	38	3¾	4
Examples: ammonium	1,220	28	2¾	3
phosphates, superphos-	1,000	23	2¼	2½
phates, mixed ferti-			Ounces	
lizers (5-10-5, 10-6-4,	785	18	30	2
10-10-10, etc.)	610	14	21	1½
	390	9	15	1
				Cups
	300	7	11	1½
	200	4¾	7½	1
	100	2¼	3½	½
			Pounds	Pints
Weight about $8/10$	1,740	40	4	5
that of water	650	15	1½	2
Examples: aluminum			Ounces	Cups

TABLE 1 *(continued)*

Materials	Weights specified per -			Volume Measure for 100 Sq. Ft.
	Acre	1,000 Sq. Ft.	100 Sq. Ft.	
sulfate, bonemeal, magnesium sulfate (epsom salts), urea.	175	4	6½	1 Tbs.
	44	1	1½	4
			Pounds	Pints
Weight about 7/10	1,740	40	4	6
that of water	1,525	35	3½	5
Examples: activated	650	15	1½	2
sewage sludge, granu-			Ounces	
lar borax, urea-form.	300	7	11	1
				Cups
	150	3½	5½	1
			Pounds	Pints
Weight about 6/10	1,300	30	3	5
that of water	545	12½	1¼	2
Examples: cottonseed			Ounces	
meal, fish scrap,	260	6	10	1
sulfur, tankage.				Cups
	130	3	5	1
			Pounds	Pints
Weight about 5/10	1,100	25	2½	5
that of water	435	10	1	2
Example: hydrated			Ounces	
lime	220	5	8	1
				Cups
	110	2½	4	1
Manure (moist):	Tons		Pounds	Bushels
loose	13	600	60	2
packed	13	600	60	1
Dry straw or leaves packed tightly with hands	5	250	25	2

Courtesy of U.S. Department of Agriculture

138

TABLE 2

FERTILIZERS, APPROXIMATE EQUIVALENT-VOLUME OF MATERIALS TO USE IN THE ROW AND PER PLANT AT VARIOUS RATES PER 100 SQUARE FEET.

Rates per 100 Square Ft.	Rates per 10 feet			Rates per plant		
	rows spaced			spaced		
	3 ft.	2 ft.	1 ft.	5 x 5 ft.	2¼ x 2¼	2 x 1½ ft.
Pints	Pints	Pints	Pints	Pints	Cups	Cups
10	3	2	1	2½	1	½
	Cups	Cups	Cups	Cups		
6	3½	2½	1¼	3	½	¼
5	3	2	1	2½	½	¼
					Tbs.	Tbs.
4	2½	1½	¾	2	6½	3
3	1¾	1¼	½	1½	5	2½
2½	1½	1	½	1¼	4	2
			Tbs.			
2	1¼	¾	6½	1	3¼	1½
1½	¾	½	5	¾	2½	1
		Tbs.				Tsp.
1	½	6	3¼	½	1½	2½
Cups				Tbs.		
1½	½	5	2½	6	1	1½
	Tbs.				Tsp.	
1	5	3¼	1½	4	2½	¾
½	2½	1½	¾	2	1¼	½
Tbs.		Tsp.	Tsp.			
4	1¼	2½	1¼	1	½	¼
	Tsp.					
1	1	½	⅓	¼	⅙	1/12
Bushels	Bushels	Pecks	Quarts	Bushel	Quarts	Quarts
2	½	1½	6	½	3	1½
	Peck			Peck		
1	1	1	3	1	1½	¾

Courtesy of U.S. Department of Agriculture

139

Mixing Liquid Fertilizers

Dried blood (12 % nitrogen) 4 teaspoons per gallon of water. Steamed bone meal (11 % phosphorus) 1 tablespoon per gallon of water.

Complete fertilizer (such as 10-10-10) 2 tablespoons per gallon of water.

Ground limestone 2 tablespoons per gallon of water. Muriate of potash (50 % potash) ½ teaspoon per gallon of water.

Nitrate of soda (16 % nitrogen) 1 tablespoon per gallon of water.

Cow manure (well-rotted) 1 dry quart to 2 gallons of water.

Hen manure (guano) 1 dry pound to 5 gallons of water.

Horse and cow manure must be stirred once or twice a day for a week before they are ready to use. Fertilizing with liquid manure or other liquid fertilizers is done the same way as watering, except that none of it must be allowed to touch the foliage. Liquid fertilizers and manures are readily absorbed by the plants' roots structures. Using liquid fertilizer is the quickest way to apply plant nutrients to the soil and thus to the plant itself.

Appendix C

Vegetable Garden Guide

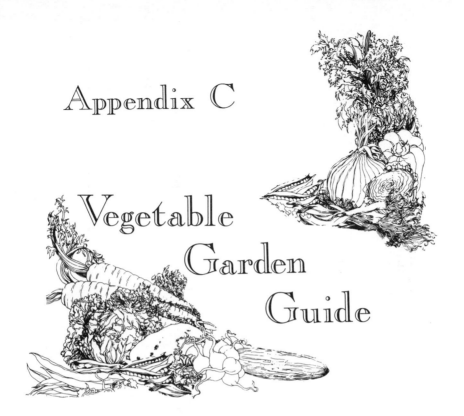

BURPEE VEGETABLE GARDEN GUIDE FOR FAMILY OF FOUR

Vegetable and types	Hardi-ness	Days to germinate	Growing suggestions	Quantity to grow	Days to harvest	Satisfactory pH range	Uses
BEAN, Snap Bush, and Pole (green and yellow)	T	7-14	Sow bush types every 2 weeks until midsummer. Support pole types.	Bush—50 ft. Pole—8 hills	50-70	5.5-6.7	Fresh, frozen, canned. Vitamins A, B, C.
BEAN, Bush, Shell (red, white and green)	T	7-14	Fava or English Broad. Bean hardier than other types. Sow as early in spring as soil can be worked.	50 ft.	65-103	5.5-6.7	Fresh shell beans, or use dried for baking, soup, or Spanish or Mexican dishes. Vitamins A, B, C.
BEAN, Lima, Bush, and Pole	T	7-14	Wait until ground is thoroughly warm before planting. Bush types mature earlier. Support pole varieties.	Bush—70 ft. Pole—8 hills	65-92	6.0-6.7	Fresh, frozen, canned, dried for baking. Vitamins A, B, C.

HH – Half Hardy Varieties
T – Tender Varieties
H – Hardy Varieties

142

BURPEE VEGETABLE GARDEN GUIDE FOR FAMILY OF FOUR

Vegetable and types	Hardi-ness	Days to germinate	Growing suggestions	Quantity to grow	Days to harvest	Satisfactory pH range	Uses
BEETS, Red, golden, white.	HH	10-21	For continuous harvest, make successive sowings until early summer. Do not transplant. This may cause forked or split roots.	25 ft.	55-80	6.0-7.5	Fresh, pickled, canned. Cook "thinnings" first, and tops later on for delicious greens. Vitamins A, B, C.
BROCCOLI	H	10-21	Plant again in mid-summer for fall harvest. Grows best in cool weather.	25-40 Plants	60-85*	5.5-6.7	Fresh, frozen. Vitamins A, B, C.
BRUSSELS SPROUTS	H	10-21	Pick lowest "sprouts" on stem each time; break off accompanying leaves but do not remove top foliage.	25-40 Plants	80-90*	5.5-6.7	Light frost improves flavor. Sprouts delicious fresh or frozen. Vitamins A, B, C.

*Time from when plants are set into garden.

143

BURPEE VEGETABLE GARGEN GUIDE FOR FAMILY OF FOUR

Vegetable and types	Hardi-ness	Days to germinate	Growing suggestions	Quantity to grow	Days to harvest	Satisfactory pH range	Uses
CABBAGE, Early, late. Red, green.	HH	10-21	Do not plant where any of the cabbage family grew the previous year.	25-40 Plants	60-110*	5.5-6.7	Fresh, salads, coleslaw, sour-kraut. Winter storage. Vitamins A, B, C.
CARROT Long, short	HH	7-14	Short root types best for shallow or heavy soil. Plant again in mid-summer for fall harvest.	25-30 ft.	65-75	5.2-6.7	Salads, relish, juice, stews, soup. Vitamins A, B, C.
CAULI-FLOWER White, purple	HH	10-21	Tie leaves over heads to whiten.	30-36 Plants	50-85*	6.0-6.7	Fresh, frozen; salad, relish. Vitamins A, B, C.
CELERY	HH	10-21	To whiten, mound soil up around mature stalks.	30-36 Plants	115-135*	5.5-6.7	Raw in salads and as relish. Cooked and creamed, sauces, soups. Vitamin A.

144

Vegetable and types	Hardi-ness	Days to germinate	Growing suggestions	Quantity to grow	Days to harvest	Satisfactory pH range	Uses
CHARD, Red or White Stalked	HH	7-14	Pick frequently to encourage fresh leaves. Stands summer heat.	20-30 ft.	60	6.0-6.7	Cook leaves for "greens"; midribs and stalks like asparagus. Vitamins A, B, C.
COLLARDS	H	7-14	Easily grown non-heading cabbage-like leaves.	20-30 ft.	80	5.5-6.7	Cook leaves for "greens"; popular in south. Vitamins A, B, C.
CRESS Garden and Water	H	3-14	Sow garden or curly-cress every 2 weeks for continuous supply. Also grows well on sunny window-sill. Grow water-cress in moist shady spots or along a shallow stream.	20-30 ft.	10-50	6.0-7.0	Salads, sandwiches, garnish, seasoning. Vitamins A, B. C,

*Time from when plants are set into garden.

145

BURPEE VEGETABLE GARDEN GUIDE FOR FAMILY OF FOUR

Vegetable and types	Hardi-ness	Days to germinate	Growing suggestions	Quantity to grow	Days to harvest	Satisfactory pH range	Uses
CUCUMBERS Slicing, Pickling.	T	7-14	Grow on fence to save space. Keep picking to encourage new fruit.	8-12 hills	53-65	5.5-6.7	Salad, relish, pickles. Vitamin A.
EGGPLANT	T	10-21	Needs warm temperature—70 to 75° F. for good germination. Pick fruits when skin has high gloss.	8-12 Plants	62-75*	5.5-6.7	Delicious fried, sauteed, or in casseroles. Vitamin A.
ENDIVE	H	7-14	Grows best in cool weather.	20-30 ft.	90	6.0-7.0	Salad, greens. Hearts can be cooked and served with cream sauce or grated cheese. Vitamins A, B, C.
KALE	H	14-21	Mature plants take cold fall and winter weather. Frost improves flavor.	25-30 ft.	55-65	5.5-7.0	Chop young leaves for salads and sandwiches. Cook for greens. Vitamins A, B, C.

BURPEE VEGETABLE GARDEN GUIDE FOR FAMILY OF FOUR

Vegetable and types	Hardi-ness	Days to germinate	Growing suggestions	Quantity to grow	Days to harvest	Satisfactory pH range	Uses
KOHLRABI	HH	14-21	Grow for spring or fall crop, thrives in cool weather.	16-20 ft.	55-60	5.5-6.7	Fresh, cooked like turnips. Frozen. Vitamins A, B, C.
LEEK	H	14-21	Whiten and improve flavor by mounding soil up around mature plants.	25-40 ft.	130	5.5-6.7	Fresh in salads. Cooked in soups, stews, or creamed. Vitamins B, C.
LETTUCE, Leaf	H	7-14	Make successive sowings in spring, and another in late summer. Keep seedbed moist to get good germination for a fall crop.	25-40 ft.	40-47	6.0-7.0	Salad, sandwiches, garnish. Vitamins A, B, C.
LETTUCE, Head	H	7-14	Needs cool weather in spring or fall to head well.	25-30 ft.	65-90	6.0-7.0	Salad, sandwiches, garnish. Vitamins A, B, C.

*Time from when plants are set into garden.

BURPEE VEGETABLE GARDEN GUIDE FOR FAMILY OF FOUR

Vegetable and types	Hardi- ness	Days to germinate	Growing suggestions	Quantity to grow	Days to harvest	Satisfactory pH range	Uses
MUSTARD GREENS Fringed or Smooth Leaves	H	7-14	Grow as fall, winter, and spring crop in mild winter areas; spring and fall in North.	25-30 ft.	35-40	5.5-6.5	Greens. Vitamins A, B, C.
MELONS Cantaloupe, Crenshaw, Casaba, Honeydew, Watermelon	T	7-14	Very sensitive to frost. Black plastic mulch speeds maturity. Needs warm sunny weather when ripening for good flavor.	12-20 hills.	75-120	6.0-6.7	Fresh, frozen. Vitamins A, B, C. Ripe cantaloupes slip away easily from stems. Ripe watermelons sound dull and hollow when tapped.
OKRA Dwarf and Tall	T	7-14	Needs hot weather to mature well. Pick pods young.	16-20 ft.	52-56	6.0-7.0	Soups, stews. Vitamins A, B, C.
ONION Yellow, white	H	10-21	Grows best in fine, well-drained sandy loam soil.	50-100 ft.	95-120	5.5-6.7	Fresh salads, pickling. Vitamins B, C.

148

Vegetable and types	Hardiness	Days to germinate	Growing suggestions	Quantity to grow	Days to harvest	Satisfactory pH range	Uses
PARSLEY Curled or Plain leaves	H	14-28	Attractive edging for flower garden; pot herb on sunny windowsill in winter.	10-20 ft.	72-90	6.0-7.5	Salad, garnish, seasoning. Dries or freezes well. Vitamins A, B, C.
PEA, Dwarf, Tall	H	7-14	Plant as early as ground can be worked.	40-100 ft.	55-79	5.5-6.7	Fresh frozen, canned, dried. Vitamins A, B, C.
PEPPER Sweet, Hot	T	10-21	Needs warm temperature—70-80° F. for good germination.	8-10 Plants	60-77*	5.5-6.5	Salad, stuffed, relish, seasoning. Vitamins A, B, C.
PUMPKIN Large, Small Bush, Vine	T	7-14	For huge "contest" pumpkins, let only 1 or 2 grow per plant.	12-20 hills	95-120	5.5-6.5	Fresh, canned, frozen. Vitamins A, B, C.
RADISH Red, white, black	H	7-14	Make successive sowings until early summer; again a month before fall frost.	15-30 ft.	22-60	5.2-6.7	Relish, salad. Vitamins B, C.

*Time from when plants are set into garden.

149

BURPEE VEGETABLE GARDEN GUIDE FOR FAMILY OF FOUR

Vegetable and types	Hardi- ness	Days to germinate	Growing suggestions	Quantity to grow	Days to harvest	Satisfactory pH range	Uses
RUTABAGA	H	14-21	Grows best in cool weather.	20-30 ft.	90	5.2-6.7	Fresh. Winter storage. Vitamins B, C.
SPINACH Crinkled and Smooth	H	7-14	New Zealand and Malabar take hot weather; other varieties cool.	20-40 ft.	42-70	6.0-6.7	Greens, frozen, canned. Vitamins A, B, C.
SQUASH, Summer, Bush, Vine	T	7-14	Keep fruits picked so plants produce more.	8-12 hills	48-60	5.5-6.5	Fresh, frozen. Vitamin A.
SQUASH, Winter, Bush, Vine	T	7-14	Black plastic mulch speeds maturity.	8-12 hills	80-120	5.5-6.5	Fresh, canned, frozen. Winter storage. Vitamin A.
SUNFLOWER	T	7-14	Use for screen plant. Protect maturing heads with bags to prevent bird damage.	25-50 ft.	80	6.0-7.5	Bird, poultry seed.

BURPEE VEGETABLE GARDEN GUIDE FOR FAMILY OF FOUR

Vegetable and types	Hardi-ness	Days to germinate	Growing suggestions	Quantity to grow	Days to harvest	Satisfactory pH range	Uses
SWEET CORN White, yellow	T	7-14	Plant in blocks of short rows for good pollination and well filled ears.	50-100 ft.	63-90	5.2-6.7	Fresh, frozen, canned. Vitamins A, B, C.
TOMATO Red, pink, yellow.	T	7-14	Hybrids especially need warm temperature—70-80° F. for good germination.	16-20 Plants	52-86*	5.2-6.7	Fresh, salad, canned, juice, pickles. Vitamins A, B, C.
TURNIPS White, yellow	H	14-21	Grow best in cool weather.	20-30 ft.	35-60	5.2-6.7	Fresh, raw, or cooked. Leaves of some types for greens

*Time from when plants are set into garden.

151

Appendix D

Mail Order Sources

W. Atlee Burpee Co.
Seed Growers
Philadelphia, Pennsylvania 19132
Clinton, Iowa 52732
Riverside, California 92502

W. F. Allen Company
Strawberry Plants
Salisbury, Maryland 21801

Gurney Seed & Nursery Company
Seed & Planting Stock
Yankton, South Dakota 57078

Allcock Manufacturing Company
Havahart Traps
Ossining, New York 10562

Appendix E

Animal and Bird Control

ANIMAL AND BIRD CONTROL

Birds:	Grackles, pigeons, and sparrows leave unsightly droppings on patios, porches, and other unenclosed spaces. They also damage and destroy berries and fruit.	To keep birds out of strawberry beds and to protect fruit trees and berry bushes—cover them with Durex Anti-Bird Mesh, a lightweight, long-lasting nylon netting. Harmless to birds and plants. Allows natural passage of sun, rain, and air. Spray roosting and nuisance areas with "Bird Tanglefoot," a sticky, non-poisonous repellent. Try a Flying Disk. It whirls crazily in slightest wind, emitting bright flashes of reflected sunlight and making sharp crackling sounds.
Dogs:	Dogs like to dig in garden areas for phantom bones and to make a cool bed in the soil.	The best prevention is to fence the area. Use an approved, harmless repellent. Some last for 3 to 6 months outdoors. Chaperone is a popular brand obtainable in spray cans and Repel-O-Sticks.
Mice and Rats:	Very destructive around all stored food supplies and young fruit trees.	Poison them with d-con. Full directions are on the label. Highly effective and easy to use. For an occasional stray mouse indoors use a snapback mouse trap baited with cheese or bacon.
Moles:	Burrowing for grubs and insects, they dislodge plant roots and cause loss of moisture. Sometimes the plants wither and die.	Treat area with Chlordane 10-G to destroy grubs and insect life on which moles depend for food.
Rabbits:	Girdle and kill fruit trees and shrubs in the winter when snows are deep and their source of food is scarce.	Wrap trunks of trees and stems of plants and shrubs with aluminum foil or burlap netting. Wrapping, to be effective, must be as high as deepest snowfall, plus height of rabbit. Live trap them with a Havahart trap.

Raccoon: Love sweet corn and will positively devastate a small patch the very first night the corn becomes ready for table use. They survey the corn patch and "stake it out" long before the corn is ripe.

Trap with Havahart trap for destruction or transport to a distant point for release. Check local trapping laws. Outline perimeter of corn patch with stakes about 18 inches tall. Tie heavy, coarse rags to tops of stakes. Each evening, saturate rags with kerosene. Raccoons will not pass this objectionable, olfactory barrier.

Snakes: Although repulsive and frightening to most people, about 99% of those encountered are harmless.

The best prevention is a clean area where they cannot find shelter and shade beneath rockpiles, boards, and other trash. Can be killed quite easily with a garden hoe. Width of blade allows a comfortable margin for error in striking the blow. Even a light blow will immobilize a snake.

Squirrels: Become attic residents unless air vents are screened.

May be live-trapped with Havahart traps. Either destroy or transport to nearest woodland and release unharmed.

Skunk: (Polecat) Nocturnal prowlers looking for insects and grubworms. They dig unsightly holes in lawns and gardens.

No grubworm, no skunks! So grubproof the area with Chlordane 10-G. May be live-trapped with Havahart traps and safely transported (in the trap) to a distant area for release.

Woodchuck: (Groundhog) Come out of their hibernation in early spring and ravenously devour young, tender vegetation. Especially destructive on young beans, cabbage, and lettuce.

A small mesh wire fence is the only sure protection. A morning, noon, and early evening vigil with a 12 ga. shotgun, using No. 4 shot, can be effective. Consult Game Warden on applicable regulations. May also be trapped with Havahart traps.

157

Appendix F

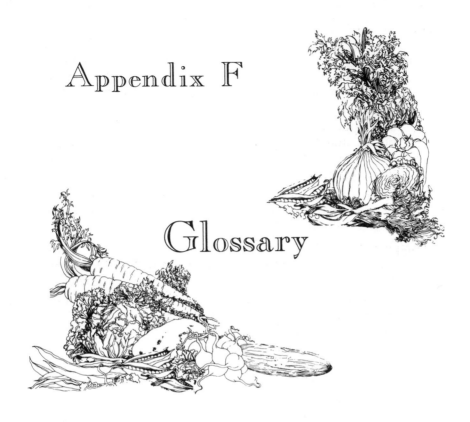

Glossary

Annual—a plant that grows from seed, blooms, and dies in one season.

Anthracnose—a distructive disease, caused by fungi, which attacks the grape, bean, cotton, melon, and other plants.

Biennial—a plant that requires two years from seed to bloom, and dies after blooming the second year.

Blanch—to bleach (celery, endive, etc.) by keeping the leaves or stalk of a plant from the light, to improve the texture and flavor.

Burrow—a hollow place in the earth dug by an animal.

Chlorophyl—the green coloring matter contained in plants; in the presence of sunlight it converts carbon dioxide and water into carbohydrates.

Compost—a man-made substitute for manure. It is made up of a wide variety of fermented and decomposed organic materials. It is an excellent source of humus and plant nutrients.

Cover Crop—a temporary crop that may be used to prevent erosion, bring leached nutrients back to the surface for new plants, stimulate biochemical processes, increase absorption of rainwater, increase organic soil matter, and increase fertility of the soil.

Cultivation—this term can apply to cultiation of a vegetable crop or to cultivation of the soil. Prime objectives are conservation of soil moisture and weed control.

Damping-Off—a term applied to the death of seedlings which topple over because the stem has rotted through at the surface of the soil.

Deciduous—falling, not persistent. A term used to describe most broad-leaved trees, which drop their leaves annually.

Decomposition—the breaking down or decay of fibrous, organic materials or similar substances.

Dolomite—rock consisting mainly of magnesium carbonate and calcium carbonate; limestone or marble with much magnesium carbonate in it.

Drill—a small trench for planting seeds. Make the drill immediately before planting to prevent sun-baking and drying out of the soil.

Forcing—the process of inducing a plant to grow faster than normal, or out of regular season. This is done by use of extra heat, light, fertilizer, or moisture.

Friable—easily crumbled or pulverized. A term used to describe soil that is easily cultivated.

Furrow—a narrow groove in the earth made by a plow or garden tool.

Fusarium Wilt—a disease of tomato plants causing yellow and dead leaves on lower part of plant. Brown streaks just under surface of stem also confirms presence of this disease.

Gene—any of the elements by which hereditary characters are transmitted and determined.

Green Manure—a term used to describe the plowing under of quick-growing, succulent crops to add humus and fertility to the soil.

Hardening Off—the process of adapting plants to withstand lower temperatures after being grown indoors. This is accomplished by less watering and gradual exposure to outdoor conditions.

Heeling In—a method of holding plants in the soil while waiting to set them out in permanent locations. Lay them in a trench with their roots lower than their tops and cover about 2/3 way to top. Water copiously to restore lost moisture in plants.

Hoeing—the new gardener should become acquainted with the two objectives of hoeing: to kill weeds and to stir or break the surface crust so the soil is open to the air and more receptive to moisture when it rains. Hoeing to a depth of 1/2 to 1 inch is deep enough to kill weeds and aerate the soil. Even though it is a simple process, one must be careful not to disturb or cut roots and stems of plants.

Humus—organic matter in an advanced stage of decomposition; excellent for aeration, water absorption, friability, and plant nutrient content of the soil.

Hybrid—a plant resulting from cross-fertilization between two or more parents differing in one or more genes.

Insecticide—any substance or preparation used to kill insects by poisoning, paralysis, or suffocation.

Intercropping—the growing of two or more crops on the same land at the same time. The system of planting different crops in alternate rows.

Iron Chelate—*chelate* means having or resembling pincer-like claws. When iron chelate is applied to the soil it remains free to be absorbed by the plant. However some iron compounds combine to form insoluble compounds in which the iron is not available to the plant.

Leaching—the loss of soluble fertilizers from the soil caused by the filtering downward of water in the ground, either from rainfall or irrigation.

Legume—any of a large group of plants of the pea family, characterized by true pods enclosing seeds; because of their ability to store up nitrates, legumes are often plowed under to fertilize the soil.

Lime—a white substance, calcium oxide, obtained by the action of heat on limestone, shells, and other material containing calcium carbonate; used in making mortar and cement and in neutralizing acid soil; also called quicklime, burnt lime, caustic lime.

Lime, hydrated—hydrated or slaked lime is burned lime to which water has been added. It should contain a minimum of 70 percent calcium oxide.

Limestone—finely ground limestone rock; at least 50 percent of it should pass through a 100-mesh screen.

Muck—black earth containing decaying matter, used as a fertilizer.

Mulch—any loose material spread on the ground around plants to prevent loss of water from the soil, to control weeds, to prevent freezing of roots, and to stabilize soil temperature. Organic mulch also adds humus and plant nutrients to the soil.

Nutrient—promoting growth, anything that nourishes. All chemical fertilizers, manures, leafmold, humus, and compost provide nutrients for plants.

Open-pollinated—a horticultural term applied to plants that are pollinated by nature in the form of plant movement, action of wind, birds, and insects.

Organic materials—any substance that once had life; that which is derived from living organisms.

Peat—partially decayed, moisture-absorbing plant matter found in ancient bogs and swamps, used as a mulch or soil conditioner.

Peat moss—a term used to describe a mulch prepared from the peat from ancient sphagnum bogs.

Perennial—a plant that has a life cycle longer than two years.

Perlite—a sterile, seed-growing medium obtained from volcanic ash.

Repellent—any substance used to repel or drive away plant pests, insects, animals, and birds.

Seedling—a term usually applied to very young plants grown from seed, as distinguished from plants propagated from cuttings, buddings, layering, etc.

Sphagnum moss—ideal, sterile medium for germination of seed. Completely eliminates damping-off. Seedlings can be easily removed with no root damage.

Stolon—a slender branch or shoot, above or below ground, which takes root at the tip and develops a new plant.

Superphosphate—a mixture of monocalcium phosphate and calcium sulfate made by treating phosphate rock with sulfuric acid.

Top dressing—an application of chemical fertilizer, manure, humus, or compost to the surface of the soil to feed plants. Best results are obtained by cultivating or raking it into the soil.

Umbel—a flower cluster spreading from a common center with the individual flower stalks being of almost equal lengths. The clusters are usually flat or convex on top. Parsley is a good example.

Vermiculite—a sterile, seed-growing medium obtained from a mica-like ore. It is light in weight, retains moisture, and permits good plant aeration. It eliminates damping-off.

Index